"Luis is a sound leader and subject matter expert who has had a bright international career. I have known him for more than ten years, and he continues to be my go-to person to get the latest updates on the payment industry, offering great insights into the up-to-the-minute market trends and how they can benefit the corporate world."

— Victor Pausin | Treasurer, North America,
Nissan Motor Co., Ltd

"Luis Guerra is a dedicated husband, father, and professional with deep roots in family and religious values. He believes in productive work and faces life with an honest, positive and energic attitude. I am honored to call Luis a friend as he acts as a role model for many of us."

— Juan C. Neuman | Financial Services
Representative, Coastal Wealth, a MassMutual Firm

"Luis is an inspiration; he constantly strives to do more and improve. He is not afraid to try new things and looks to the future without losing track of the moment. He is willing to help anyone and everyone. Luis has been working at Visa for a very long time. He is constantly striving to learn more and develop relationships with others. As a friend, Luis is a great listener and an empathetic person concerned with everyone's well-being. His kindness and smile are contagious. Luis practices his faith and shares his faith with others. His messages to me constantly remind me to pray and rarely ever go without an ending of God Bless. As practicing Catholics, we are all called to evangelize. Luis does this by not being afraid to talk about his faith - to live his faith every day."

— Lawrence Franzoni | Husband, Father,
and Knights of Columbus 12240 – Chancellor

"Luis Guerra is constantly demonstrating leadership with creativeness. What I like the most is that he stays hungry and is always hustling. His perspective and enthusiasm make him a person you must meet in person."

— Luis G. Castillo | Founder/Owner Global Trade Insurance,
Registered Broker of Eximbank of USA,
Eximbank of US is a Federal Agency of USA

"As a leader with everlasting stamina, Luis has successfully established himself as a key executive in the financial industry across the Americas, but what is most important is that he has been able to raise an outstanding family. Always with a smile and a will of service, he has been able to accomplish and surpass unimaginable goals in the markets where he has worked. His work is a must-read for anybody who is looking forward to building a successful career path."

— Juan Carlos Sanchez | Multiplatform Media Strategist, Telemundo

"Luis is a great friend, actually more than that. I consider him a brother. He is honest, trustworthy, a man of faith, and the person with whom I was very close to joining forces in a business partnership. Luis is also a dear husband and a great father of three beautiful children. It is an honor to be able to say that not only I know Luis Guerra, but also that God has crossed our paths and I consider him my brother. My Hermanazo! Like I actually call him."

— Max Biella | Sales Manager, Tri Meats., Inc

BEYOND SUCCESS

with

LUIS GUERRA

Also Featuring
Other Top Authors

© 2019 Success Publishing

Success Publishing, LLC
2810 Trinity Mills, #209-221
Carrollton, Texas USA 75006
questions@mattmorris.com

All rights reserved. No part of this book may be reproduced, stored in a retrieval system, or transmitted in any form or by any means - electronic or mechanical, photocopy, recording, or any other - except for brief quotations in printed reviews, without the prior permission of the publisher. Although the author(s) and publisher have made every effort to ensure the accuracy and completeness of information contained in this book, we assume no responsibility for errors, inaccuracies, omissions, or any inconsistency herein.

Table of Contents

CHAPTER 1
PRAY HARD WORK HARD: A ROUTE FOR ACHIEVING
SUCCESS AND HAPPINESS IN LIFE
BY LUIS GUERRA.. 9

CHAPTER 2
THE POWER OF MANIFESTATION
BY MATT MORRIS 15

CHAPTER 3
THE PERSON YOU COULD HAVE BEEN
BY STEVE MORELAND 19

CHAPTER 4
SUCCESS IS BEING ABLE TO LIVE A LIFE OF PRIORITIES
NOT OBLIGATIONS
BY DR. JIM STORHOK 26

CHAPTER 5
KEY TO SUCCESS IS FOCUS
BY JASON REID... 32

CHAPTER 6
ROADBLOCKS IN LIFE COME FROM OUR MINDSET
BY ROBERT BUCKO 37

CHAPTER 7
HOW I WENT THROUGH THE LOWEST OF LOWS TO
BECOME SUCCESSFUL
BY JAMIE LESTER 44

CHAPTER 8
FEAR AND SELF-DOUBT TO FEELING GOOD IN MY
OWN BODY

BY ADDA HAFBORG 49

CHAPTER 9
WHAT MAKES SOME PEOPLE MORE SUCCESSFUL THAN OTHERS?
BY MAXWELL ADEKOJE 55

CHAPTER 10
THE FIRST TIME I FAILED IN MY LIFE WAS THE DAY I WAS BORN
BY KATE JONES 62

CHAPTER 11
REDEFINING MY DEFINITION OF SUCCESS
BY ARLENE BINOYA-STRUGAR, PSY.D. 68

CHAPTER 12
5 STEPS TO BECOMING A GOOD ENTREPRENEUR
BY JASMINA CERNILOGAR MIHAJLOVIC 73

CHAPTER 13
LIVING AN INSPIRED, PURPOSEFUL, AND AMAZING LIFE
BY JEREMY HOORT 78

CHAPTER 14
I AM NOTHING. YET, I HAVE EVERYTHING
BY MAIKO JOHANSON 84

CHAPTER 15
HOW TO WORK LESS, EARN MORE AND LIVE FREE AS A LIFESTYLE ENTREPRENEUR
BY FRANCIS ABLOLA 89

CHAPTER 16
YOUR PARTNER IN CRIME: THE SUBCONSCIOUS MIND
BY OLIVER T. ASAAH 94

CHAPTER 17
THE JOURNEY OF SUCCESS
BY DR. STEVEN & DR. TERRESA BALESTRACCI 101

CHAPTER 18
ESSENTIAL SUCCESS: "A LIVING TRANSFORMATION"
BY RAY BLANCHARD, PH.D. 107

CHAPTER 19
REACHING SUCCESS WITH EXCELLENCE
BY ELLEN REID.. 114

CHAPTER 20
BECOMING THE MAN IN THE ARENA
BY MIKEL ERDMAN 119

CHAPTER 21
INSPIRATION WHEN YOU LEAST EXPECT IT
BY BRIAN MAHANY 127

CHAPTER 22
WHAT LEGACY ARE YOU GOING TO LEAVE BEHIND?
BY JILL NIEMAN PICERNO... 133

CHAPTER 23
MY SUCCESS IS ACHIEVED BY CREATING STRONG
RELATIONSHIPS
BY ANDRE' SERRAILE... 139

CHAPTER 24
THE DANCE LIFE
BY BLAKE ELDER 147

CHAPTER 25
RESCUED INTO MANHOOD
BY FRANK MBANUSI.. 158

CHAPTER 26
MY DEFINITION OF SUCCESS
BY KADRI KRISTELLE KARU 164

CHAPTER 27
WINNING THROUGH THE WRINKLES IN LIFE
BY LaShonda McMorris 171

CHAPTER 28
YOU MIGHT SCREAM, YOU MIGHT CRY, BUT GIVING UP IS NOT AN OPTION
BY MAGGA SIGGA 178

CHAPTER 29
THE 5 PRINCIPLES OF NETWORKING
BY NICHOLAS ARBUTINA 183

CHAPTER 30
TRIUMPH THROUGH A BUMPY ROAD
BY JAMES MBELE 189

CHAPTER 31
RULE YOUR MIND, ROCK YOUR BEST LIFE
BY STEPH SHINABERY 195

Chapter 1

PRAY HARD WORK HARD: A ROUTE FOR ACHIEVING SUCCESS AND HAPPINESS IN LIFE

By Luis Guerra

I am the oldest of four children; born and raised in Venezuela. My father is the main inspiration for all my efforts aimed towards achieving personal excellence in life. He was a two-time cabinet member under two different Venezuelan governments, and he obtained two Masters Degrees in Law from the University of Rome and New York, as well as attaining his Ph.D. from Harvard University. How can one not be inspired by someone like that?

My father is the oldest of seven children, and he was seventeen when his father died. Being the oldest, he had to assume the role as head of the family and provide for six children. They were a lower-middle-income class Venezuelan family with no excess of economic resources. I didn't have the chance to know my grandpa, but my father told me he was a hard-working man in the construction business. My grandmother was a saint by nature who lived a calm and pure life and died at the age of ninety- three of natural causes.

At seventy-seven years of age, my Dad continues to challenge himself by continuously exploring new professional projects and goals, and in the last five years, he authored four books on Constitutional Law. When I say to him, "Dad, I think it's time for you to slow down," he always provides the same answer, "I just won't be only walking a dog around the neighborhood and sustain my living standards by rental income out of my properties."

My mother married my father when she was only eighteen years old. He took her to Italy when he did his first Master's degree in Law, and she had the great opportunity to learn Italian. She has a natural ability to learn different languages. Maybe it's because she has an ear for music and rhythm. Every time we go to an Italian restaurant, she speaks fluent Italian with the owner and waitresses. It is admirable. My mom is my inspiration for the steadfast belief in prayer. The moment you meet her, you immediately notice she is a person with God at the bottom of her heart who has a perceptible love for life.

Mom is the oldest of six children and was raised by the best grandparents I could ever have. I don't remember my grandfather being depressed or down about anything in life. My grandmother, even though she had a bitter temperament, was a world-record prayer. Yes, it's the truth. During my teens, I remember her almost falling asleep on her rocking chair every night trying to finish reading all her prayers (more than ten, easily) and praying the Rosary.

I am the father of three children or the beneficiary of three miracles. Yes, for those that don't believe in miracles, being able to procreate through God's will is a miracle. There's no doubt about it. Two beautiful daughters and a son are my miracles. My close friends sometimes like to call me the United Nations. You want to know why? I left my home country, Venezuela, in 2008, because of my job. I was transferred to Santiago de Chile. My oldest daughter was only 11 months old at the time. We lived in Chile for nearly five years and our second daughter was born there. I was then transferred to Miami-USA, where my son was born.

As you can see, we're the perfect example of a family that practices globalization and unites nations. I have two master's degrees. One in International Economics and Finance from Brandeis University and an Executive MBA from Universidad Adolfo Ibanez, which I completed while working in Chile.

I married a beautiful woman. My wife is also one of my main inspirations for hard work. I met her while she was an intern working for me. Isn't that funny? Long story short, we ended up getting married after dating for about two years (of course, after she finished her internship and went to work for another company). We are the parents of three blessings; our three children. My wife did her Master's degree in Finance, not only while on the job but when she was pregnant with our first daughter. And today, she continues to have a full-time job and puts all her efforts in as a mother and wife while always having that million-dollar smile that made me fall in love with her seventeen years ago.

So, what is all this Pray Hard Work Hard philosophy about? It all started during a seminar about "Virtuous Leadership: An Agenda for Personal Excellence." I realized then the tremendous power and value that God can imprint on our lives if we put into practice one of God's most precious gifts to humankind, The Cardinal Virtues. Whether you're a firefighter, head of government, a department secretary, successful businessman, famous sports player, rock star, housewife or nanny, you can exercise leadership if you put the Cardinal Virtues into practice: Humility, Magnanimity, Prudence, Courage, Self-Control, and Justice. Humility and Magnanimity set the foundation for the other four. To practice the virtue of Humility, you need to have the ambition to serve others. To practice Magnanimity, you need to have the ambition to conduct all your efforts towards achieving great things in life. I will get into each of the other four in more detail as we move through the chapter.

The Latin phrase "Sine Me nihil potestis facere" means "Without Me, you cannot do anything by yourself." It was frequently used by Saint Jose Maria Escriva, founder of the Roman-Catholic prelature Opus Dei (Work of God), whose mission statement is to help people become saints through professional work and in the ordinary life events (being a good father, husband, friend, brother or sister, co-worker, employee, etc.). We don't have to do extraordinary things to become saints. When learning about this Latin phrase, I began to look at the way I lived my ordinary and professional life in a completely different way. In the phrase, the word "Me" refers to God and invites anyone to remain humble, no matter the position or power you have in society. It automatically prevents arrogance and reminds us that we are in this world for a limited period. It helps you to detach from material things and not only strive for financial success but also to help others. Finally, it invites you to develop a close friendship with God by praying every day.

I allocate short periods throughout the day to pray. It can be calling God to give me strength and will to finish my work in the best way possible, or it can be praying Our Father or the Hail Mary. When I arrive at the office each morning, I imagine myself in a field where I need to chase God all day long to serve Him, my clients, my colleagues, or anybody. In soccer terms, it's like putting all my energy into running around the soccer field chasing God as if He was the soccer ball and trying to score as many goals as I can. There might be days where I don't run as fast as I would love to, but I always run. I don't stop running. My Monday mornings have become a Friday morning where all of us are thrilled and eager to start enjoying the weekend with our family and friends.

Virtuous leaders put all their effort into achieving personal excellence in everything they do. They are continually searching for new challenges that lead to serving others as God (Jesus Christ) always does. Put in another way, invite Jesus Christ to become part of your working team of executives, managers, analysts, administrative assistants, etc, and I guarantee that you will make sure you do your job the best you can to serve Him. You will immediately avoid mediocracy; you will never give up no matter the obstacles, pitfalls, and challenges you face in your daily life. You will always remember the suffering God endured on the cross to redeem our sins, and you will start to act like an eagle and not like a chicken. You will suddenly become and be seen as a natural leader and inspiration for others around you.

Let me share an example of what I mean when I say invite Jesus Christ to be part of your working team and to start acting like an eagle and stop acting like a chicken. I used to have a pretty tough and arrogant client. For those of you who work in sales as relationship managers, the situation will sound familiar. You could have the same situation with a co-worker or even with your supervisor. But, going back to my story, I tried to offer this client the best service possible, and he was never 100% satisfied.

Additionally, if something went wrong, he would humiliate not only you but your team members too and make us feel like cockroaches. We both agreed on having bi-weekly touch base calls, and when the date was approaching, I started to feel nervous, uncomfortable, and anxious. Once I began to establish a close relationship with God and prayed before each of those calls, I would tell myself I had to put all my sacrifice into this to serve Him as He did it for me while on the cross. The situation changed dramatically. I stopped dragging my feet when it came to making the call, and even the conversations started to turn in the right direction. My client started to follow me instead of me following him. I began to practice the virtue of self-control, which now leads me to explain what it really means to be self-controlled.

Everything in life, including self-control and leadership, is learned. Nobody is born with it. You need to learn to control your temperance, master your passions, emotions, feelings and not let them master you. In my client's case, what do you think I wanted to do with him? I wanted to hang up the phone, finish the conversation at once and insult him with any bad word that could come to mind. Self-control goes hand-in-hand with the virtue of humility. By being humble and reminding myself that I was to serve him, I was eventually able to establish a good relationship with him — an association governed by respect and credibility. I didn't take it personally. I didn't feel rejected by him.

In my daily work life, I encounter stressful situations. Important decisions need to be made, and I am accountable for any mistakes. If a deal goes wrong because of my fault, I will get hit. There are no excuses for blaming others. This is where I practice the Cardinal Virtue of Prudence. Having prudence is having the ability to make the right decisions.

Ensure you are deliberate and gather all relevant information, judge the information, and consider the different opinions. Finally, decide which is the best route to follow according to your perception. When you are deliberate, you are considering all the facts, the reality, whereas the decision-making has to do with will and action.

One of my favorite Cardinal Virtues is Courage. Why? Because when you practice it, you are putting yourself in a situation where you always need to stick to your moral values. As we know, in life, we're often faced with temptation. Whether it's as simple as controlling your food or alcohol intake, or making a tough business decision for the good of your employees, God will knock at your heart and soul and will tell you, "Hey my dear friend, stay on course, and don't let them influence you in a bad way". Instead, always act like an eagle and not like a chicken. Each of us has the responsibility to keep our ears wide open to listen to God's words and take the appropriate action. We need to have the courage to tell people in a good way when they're wrong. Try it, and you'll feel 100% fulfilled.

Finally, I'd like to explain the Cardinal Virtue of Justice. As Alexandre Havard defines, "It is the habit of giving others their due, not merely now and then, but always." A just person is always concerned about doing good while he or she walks through their life. We have a unique opportunity to do good at work.

Making the time to help a co-worker, servicing our clients with the right attitude, congratulating an employee for a job well done, and listening enthusiastically to a family member after a long day at work, are opportunities that God puts in front of us to practice the virtue of Justice.

I hope you all have found this chapter useful to improve work performance, become better citizens, and help you develop a real and close relationship with God. I invite each one of you to start making your Mondays a Friday where we set our clocks to countdown from ten to zero and once at zero, run to our houses to start enjoying the weekend with our family and friends. We live only once!

God Bless you all!

Biography

Luis Guerra has more than 15 years of experience as a relationship manager in the banking and technology payments industry. He has worked in more than ten markets across Latin America and the Caribbean. He holds a Master of Arts in International Economics and Finance from Brandeis University and an Executive MBA from Universidad Adolfo Ibanez. Luis is an active Catholic, known for his perseverance in the workspace.

Contact Information

Facebook: https://www.facebook.com/luis.e.guerra.9
Instagram: https://www.instagram.com/luiseguerra72

Chapter 2
THE POWER OF MANIFESTATION

By Matt Morris

It had been about three days since my last bath. Not that you could even call it a bath. Every two or three days, I would find a gas station bathroom that would lock from the inside. I'd take off all my clothes, splash water up from the sink, soap up, and then splash water to rinse off. I remember always praying that no one would be waiting outside because the floor would be soaking wet.

I had completely run out of money. I had also run out of credit. I was approximately $30,000 in debt and couldn't even make the minimum payments on my credit cards. I had been forced to live out of my car because I couldn't afford rent or even $20 a night to stay in a sleazy motel. I was selling above ground swimming pools in southern Louisiana during the two hottest months of the year and didn't get paid commissions until the pool got installed six to eight weeks later. So, for two months, my Honda Civic was my home sweet home.

Sitting all alone in my car that night, I was overly aware that my life had hit rock bottom. Not only was I lonely, broke and living out of my car, but I had just showered naked in the rain in the church parking lot in which I was parked. To be specific, I had showered under the gutter runoff from the roof of the church.

The burning question in my mind that night was, "How?" How in the world had I gotten myself into this situation? I knew I wasn't there because of a lack of effort or even a lack of intelligence. (I wasn't lazy, and I actually considered myself to be a pretty smart guy.)

After experiencing both utter failure and extreme success in my life, I have become acutely aware of what exactly manifested that situation. I'm also aware of what has now allowed me to become a self-made millionaire, travel around the world to over 50 countries, become a best-selling author and speaker attracting audiences of thousands every year.

You might think what caused those results were the *actions* leading up to them because, as we know, every action does produce a result. Most people focus only on the "how to's" but never seem to achieve their full potential because the decision to take proper or improper actions is a byproduct of your original intention. If the intention is not set properly, one will almost always make the wrong decisions on what actions to take which, in turn, lead to an undesired result.

What lies at the heart of manifesting your full potential is your intention.

What is intention? The dictionary defines it as the end or objective intended or purpose. While that sounds incredibly simple, utilizing the power of intention needs a bit more clarification of how you truly manifest that purpose for yourself.

An intention is your inner belief of what is already present but has simply not manifested in physical form yet. A true intention comes with the commitment and honest belief that anything else is an absolute impossibility. You see, when you're committed to a result, it's already done. Without it already being done in your mind, it cannot be considered a true intention but simply a fleeting wish.

When it comes to achieving your result, the simplest and widely accepted model for you to follow is what we call *cause and effect*. Think of your result as your effect. Your job is to identify and create the cause that will produce your effect.

Most people naturally assume that the cause is the physical actions or the steps you need to take to get your desired effect. What I'm proposing to you here, however, is that the series of action steps is not the real cause. The actions are really part of the effect.

So, the question is then, what's the cause?

The real cause is the intention you made to create that effect in the first place. The moment you say to yourself, "let it be so," is the real cause. Without the decision or your intention, the effect will never manifest. Your intention is ultimately what causes everything in your life to manifest.

If you want to achieve a goal, the most crucial part is to *decide* to manifest it. It doesn't matter if you feel it's out of your capabilities to achieve it. It doesn't matter if you can't see *how* you're going to achieve it. The *how* is insignificant because the universe will usually never manifest the *how* until *after* you've made the decision.

If you look at the origin of the word "decide," it is actually "to cut off." Your "decision" then should be framed in your mind as cutting off any other option other than your desired result. If failure is an option in your mind, your true intention is actually failure.

So step 1 is to *decide* not to wonder if you can do it and not to think of all the reasons that are holding you back. If you want to start your own business, then decide to make it so first. If you want to get married, decide to attract a mate. Whatever it is you want out of life, make a decision and a commitment *first,* and *then* work out the *how.*

If you have doubts in your head, you will find doubts in the world. You see, my belief is that the universe can sense a lack of commitment to a goal. It's like those people who say they are going to *try* to do something and *see how it goes.* When you come from a place of uncertainty or if you're wishy-washy about your goal, then the universe is not going to help you achieve it.

When you have total certainty in declaring your intention, you attract people like a magnet. When you are energized, motivated and have declared your goal to be so, that resonates in your being, and the universe aligns itself to work with you to manifest your intention.

You must also realize that your subconscious mind is infinitely more powerful than your conscious mind and that your subconscious mind controls your outcome 100%. When you are uncertain consciously about your goal, your subconscious does everything in its power to hold you back. You see, your subconscious acts like a computer. It accepts 100% of the data your conscious mind gives it. When your conscious mind feeds it negativity, it produces negative results for you. When your conscious mind feeds it excitement, positivity, and certainty, it produces all the energy and creativity it possibly can to ensure that you accomplish your intended result.

If you want to achieve any goal, your first step is to declare it and then to clear out all words like "hopefully," "can't," "maybe" and the killer - "try." When someone tells me they're going to "try" to do something, I know that they're *not* going to do it.

Such words are all signs of a lack of commitment, that you don't believe in yourself and that you're using your own power against yourself. You see, we all have the same amount of power – it's just deciding if we want to use our power negatively or positively. When you use your power negatively, you're saying, "let me be powerless." If you think weakness, you manifest weakness. If you project certainty, you manifest certainty.

"Energy flows where attention goes."

You get whatever you think about most often. Whatever you think about expands. Therefore, we must constantly focus on what we want!

Remember, "we" create our destiny by the committed focus of our intention.

Biography

Author of the International Bestselling *The Unemployed Millionaire*, Matt Morris began as a serial entrepreneur at 18. Since then, he has generated over $1.5 billion through his sales organizations totaling over one million customers worldwide. As a self-made millionaire and one of the top Internet and Network Marketing experts, he's been featured on international radio, television and spoken from platforms to audiences in over 25 countries around the world. And now, as the founder of Success Publishing, he co-authors with leading experts from every walk of life.

Contact Information

http://www.MattMorris.com | http://successpublishing.com/

Chapter 3

THE PERSON YOU COULD HAVE BEEN

By Steve Moreland

We Texans pride ourselves on a few things. Toughness is Rule #1, and it means "no tears allowed." Our indoctrination begins the moment we arrive.

The other rules follow. Do only BIG things, especially if others say it can't be done. Rub some dirt on wherever you're bleeding; scars prove your worth. And do Right, even if the Lord God, herself, threatens you to do otherwise.

Brutal. Spartan, some would say. But definitely the kind of folks you'd want covering your back in a fight. Its belief carved deep in our soul that there is simply NO FREE LUNCH. And did I mention, we love to fight? Yep, and we don't know what that thing called a "truce" is all about.

At age twelve, I started "earning my worth." My phone rang off the wall with grass-cutting jobs in the Texas infernos called summer because my dad drilled me to deliver results beyond expectations. No excuses. Just disciplined results!

Went right to work after graduating with academic scholarships – working for three Fortune 500 companies and going to college at night. At twenty-five, I started my own brokerage firm in Dallas. By thirty, I'd made it to millionaire status, flew in private jets to do deals in European castles, hid money in numbered Swiss bank accounts, and spoke on international stages raising millions for venture capital deals.

I was Vice president of offshore operations for a boutique hedge fund based in Turks and Caicos, CEO of 58-office tax and trust firm based in Salt Lake City, and co-principal for a start-up SaaS company out of Irvine, California. Part of every month, I lived at my office in the banking district of Nassau, Bahamas, where I acted as the vice president of new business development for a middle eastern banking syndicate.

Occasionally, I woke up at a place my then-wife and children called home. And it was here that I slowed down enough to rub some of that Texas dirt on my hand, tremors that began from only sleeping on overseas flights and stumbling forward so fast everything had become a blur.

It wasn't the success, the money, the black VISA card, or the fans (though they were awesome!). It was something more insidious. Something more potent than mamby-pamby pixy dust from motivational gurus with their crybaby stories.

My dad had decreed standing orders. "You can rest when you're dead!" And this came from his creed that a man only earns a medal on his gravestone if he dies in combat. I'd been trained to fear only one thing. "Hell is meeting the person you could have been!"

And when Fate's blood-stained hurricane found me, I was ready. Ready to blindly march into Hades itself. And, like the Greek myth of Sisyphus, I remember thinking to myself, "Maybe God is not good." I recall feeling agony, real soul-crushing pain that made me wish I could just die and get it over. Wallowing in my self-pity after losing everything, I'd succumb to that state of a *victim* of Fate. And that dirt didn't fix the wounds I'd caused my family for the undeserved trials and tribulations my foolishness had caused.

Though I was brought up with my dad's relentless Marine Corp code of conduct and my mom's Christian beliefs, I doubted those beliefs. And, like the Bible's character Job, I blamed God for not protecting us from this horror. I beggingly prayed for an instant and easy fix. I just wanted that magical snap of a finger and everything to be like it used to be. But that never happens, does it?

Strength isn't forged in the cauldron of luxury and comfort. And medals don't get pinned to your uniform for holding hands and singing "Kum Ba Yah." It took time to face my demons and do the most excruciating thing I'd ever done. Take responsibility for my stupidity. Realizing that I couldn't change the past or erase what my mistakes had cost my family, I had to decide – blame others and wallow in self-pity or use hell to become better!

In school, we're first taught the lesson that prepares us for the test. But, in life, we face the Test first; later, we learn the Lesson.

The grade is what we become through it all. It's pass or fail, heaven or hell. Yes, hell is when you meet that person you could have been. But heaven is so much harder. It means rising again and again within the blood-stained hurricane of Fate. Only this repeated discipline distinguishes the few from the many, the extraordinary from the ordinary, the worthy from the worthless.

That person you could have been is only Hell if he or she stands better than you chose to become! **Hell, then, is meeting the *better* person you could have been.**

My penance for failing that critical life Test is to better our world. If Fate's blood-stained hurricane has not found your life yet, she's just hiding over the horizon, waiting until you're at your most vulnerable. If you're willing to listen to someone that knows about life's ash heap, I share the Lessons learned *after* my failed Test. They're about how thinking differently empowered me to thrive where most cannot survive. No fluffy bullshit. No rah-rah! Just what worked.

May the following battle-tested advice return you from your seemingly impossible hurricane ***"tested – and found not wanting."***

Have you ever been really curious about something? Obsessed even?

Since I was a kid, I wanted to unravel this thing called thinking. I thought to myself, if I could only understand how the few we call successful actually think, I might be able to make the world a little bit better. Because, for the most part, they are not any different than us, right? But with one exception, they see things differently in their minds.

Personal development "coaches" blather about managing our thinking. It is THE key, agreed. But it's not enough to know *what* to do. We've got to know *how* to do it. It's the subtle and often hidden difference between learning science without the art of knowing how it applies to real-world situations. Most "well-meaning" coaches deserve an "A" for science but an "F" in art. Never earning a medal from within Fate's blood-stained hurricane means their theories can only get you one place – a chance to meet the person you could have been.

Here's an example of a coach with earned rank, Dr. Viktor Frankl – author of *Man's Search For Meaning*. Frankl didn't just survive six years of Nazi concentration camps, he changed the world forever with his discovery of how we create meaning through our thinking. Better thinking creates better doing, and better doing creates a better being.

Frankl forced me to think. I mean, really think. All of a sudden, what Professor Eli Goldratt wrote in *The Goal* became crystal. "If we continue to do what we have done, which is what everybody else is doing, we will continue to get the same *unsatisfactory* result." Isn't that what we do so very often - more of what everyone else has done, expecting a different outcome?

We are what we've done, right? So, aren't our actions - what we *do* - what creates who we *become*? In short, "doing creates being." So, who we are today – our being, is a product of our past doings? Becoming someone better can only happen by doing differently. And this different had to start in the thoughts deep within.

Because I wanted a different future, one that honored the sacred by making the world better, I could no longer afford to think like everyone else. Maybe you're brighter than me and already know this. But for me, this realization was like Eureka! And instantly, I felt something deep inside.

If my prior thinking caused my current doings (my actions and habits that are known as my reality), **then why couldn't I change my future by changing the way I was thinking now?**

Socrates (Greek philosopher 470 B.C.) taught a Secret passed through to his student Plato to his student Aristotle (Greek philosopher 384 B.C.). Aristotle planted this secret into the mind of a 13-year-old prince. This secret method of thinking changed history.

At 16 years of age, the prince led his cavalry at the Battle of Chaeronea, decimating a supposedly unbeatable army. At 20 years of age, he became the king of Greece, marched his army towards Persia, solved the riddle of the Gordian Knot, destroying all who opposed. At 24, he destroyed the supposedly unconquerable city of Tyre.

At 25, he became Pharaoh of Egypt only to return to the desert near modern-day Babylon to lead his 50,000-man army against a force of 500,000 led by the Persian emperor Darius. Charging into the front line on his legendary black stallion Bucephalus, he achieved the impossible and became emperor of the known world.

By age 30, he had conquered the largest empire in history and is still studied in war colleges today for his battlefield genius, ethical governance, and unrivaled valor.

The Secret thought? "Be what you wish to seem."

The Result? One *impossible* difficulty after another - conquered!

His Name? Alexander

How is he remembered? Alexander the Great!

Hell is meeting the person you could have been, right?

So these Lessons learned after the Test lead to better actions, which lead to becoming a better being. That means that tests uncover our weaknesses so that we can learn greater lessons. What and who we became through the Tests and Lessons reflects our grade.

If we're honest, we'll admit that we often create our own storms. And then we blame others when they must be endured. But if we use the agony, we find something called grit. Grit is commitment bathed in love to become better than we were the day before. It's a relentless dedication to rise to become better, stronger, and smarter. It's a refusal to quit, even when we feel we can't get up again.

The question is, will we? Will we persist after the problems that were caused by our poor thinking – and the actions that followed? Or will we just quit due to the fear of failing, never suffering the scars that come from learning our lessons? Yeah, no easy answers. If it were easy, everyone would be the best possible version of themselves.

Those that fight to be better are never pretty. They're bloody from one battle after another. They don't know how to give up. And their scars reflect rank, how many times they returned to the chaos of the hurricane instead of hiding and waiting for the rescue that never arrives.

The Secret of "Be what you wish to seem" comes down to *"acting as if"* you've already achieved your ultimate end. What kept me marching through my blood-stained hurricane was my Gravestone, the ultimate end of what I could still become, if I changed my thinking.

Follow me. Every gravestone can fit about ten words on it. These words express how we lived, as witnessed by those that saw the real version of us, not the fake one we wear to impress others.

So, how did I *not* end up in Hell, meeting the person I could have been?

It boiled down to the little videos I saw in my mind's eye. I daily relived my greatest nightmare, experiencing it deep in my soul – again and again. The nightmare that my children chiseled on my Gravestone, "A quitter with excuses, like most." I actually saw the ceremony and those that I loved standing in silence. These words are why I refused to take the easy way out and quit.

I kept marching by visualizing, daydreaming about what I did not want to be remembered for. Sounds morbid, I know. But this propelled me to find a way to rise once more and keep moving forward, even when I felt the Lord, had abandoned me. I decided that my children would never be ashamed of their father, which caused every action to become a reason to be more, by living to do more, for others.

And on occasion, I'd dream of a moment when my children might forgive me for my poor thinking. On that good day, I'd see a different gravestone, having become that person that deserved words like "A Better World Exists Because He Determined To Think Better."

So, try my proven exercise on for size. Ask yourself the following:
1. What would your family and closest friends write on your ultimate end? (Why not ask them, if you have any guts?)
2. What do you *not* want them to chisel on your Gravestone?
3. What do you hope they will chisel on your Gravestone?

It's really simple. **How you choose to be remembered is who you will become!**

By routinely practicing this exercise, you'll be crystal clear about how to thrive within Fate's hurricane.

- You will know what actions that you cannot *do*
    - That which will cause you to become **who** you do not wish to be remembered as;
    - That which will cause you to do **what** you do not wish to be remembered for.
- You also know exactly what actions you must *do*
    - That which will cause you to become **who** you wish to be remembered as;
    - That will cause you to do **what** you wish to be remembered for.

It may be cliché, but our very thinking sparks our every action. These doings, added together over time, construct our being - *what* and *who* we become.

A short expression chiseled in stone broadcasts to a future world our *being* because of our *doings*. Did we dishonor the sacred, settling for what everybody else is doing and continuing to get their same unsatisfactory results?

Or did we ***think*** **better**, in order to ***do*** **better**, so that we could ***be*** **better**?

This is the Secret. My gift to you, as Aristotle long ago shared with Alexander, "be what you wish to seem." We become what we choose to be. It's all about our thinking.

Now you know that Hell is NOT meeting the person you could have been.

Hell is meeting the *better* person you could have been.

Biography

Steve Moreland is a native Texan known for dedicated practice and success. His Rubicon system teaches people how to perform the common under uncommon conditions. Motivated by the Latin creed FORTES FORTUNA ADIUVAT "Fortune favors the brave," his mission is to deliberately cause affirmative outcomes that would not have occurred otherwise.

Contact Information

Rubicon Website: gonerubicon.com/
Rubicon Facebook Page:
https://www.facebook.com/RubiconPerforms/
Instagram: livebravely_dieworthy
Facebook: https://www.facebook.com/steven.moreland.5205
LinkedIn: https://www.linkedin.com/in/steve-moreland-088730118/

CHAPTER 4

SUCCESS IS BEING ABLE TO LIVE A LIFE OF PRIORITIES NOT OBLIGATIONS

By Dr. Jim Storhok

Success is so many things to so many people. Perhaps it's a fat bank account, a large home with acreage, or a fancy sports car for you. Or, perhaps it's a loving marriage or a large family. For others, success is living a life of service through missionary work, public service, or growing a large, successful company. I feel all of these things are very worthy of being considered "a success." For me, my definition of success was to never "haveta." What I mean by that is that I despise having to do something when it's not in line with my priorities. It's not that I'm not grateful or feel blessed for my Doctoral education in the field of Orthopedic Physical Therapy, but I hate feeling like I "haveta" go into the office and treat patients to earn a living and provide for my family.

When we have a sick child at home, or when my wife is stressed out from being up all night with a crying, fussy infant, I always feel bad about leaving her and my family because I "haveta" provide for the family by going to a traditional 9-to-5 job. Again, to be clear, I'm honored to be able to serve my clientele in our clinic. I gain great satisfaction and take pride in the fact that I'm providing a service that can change a life by providing better physical well-being and a life with better function and less pain. However, as I've always said, I love my family MORE than I love my patients.

My priorities are 1. God, 2. Family, 3. Business, 4. Fitness/Health. My ultimate definition of success, and my reason for getting into network marketing, and more recently, digital marketing, is to be able to help others live lives based upon their priorities, not their obligations. Even more specifically, my passion is to inspire other men to want to lead their families to the best of their abilities. I'm striving to inspire other men to want to create a life from which they don't need a vacation. That's what intrigued me so much about the network marketing profession. Once you put together a sales organization properly, and back it with appropriate systems to create duplication, you can create true wealth, according to Robert Kiyosaki, successful entrepreneur and author. That translates into both time and money.

A problem that I see in society today is that we have two to three categories of men. The first type is the guy who is satisfied with putting in his hours, doing the minimum to get by and live a comfortable existence. He may raise children, but it's more like a couch potato raising the next generation of tater tots. There's lots of entertainment, watching sports and T.V., video games, and not much vision, except for maybe two weeks off for vacation (when he gets paid). Now, I don't think there's anything wrong with a little TV, playing an occasional video game, or relaxing from time to time, but I do wish that more men were striving for excellence, not just exist in the home.

The second category of men I see is comprised of men who are operating at full force, out to prove something and are striving to score big time in corporate America. They are the go-getters, willing to work 80-100 hours per week to earn enough to hit the next status symbol: move into the larger home, purchase the latest sports car and have all the toys so they "look the part." The problem here is that these men may be providing financially for their family, but at what ultimate price? These guys may be present in the home physically, but often they are preoccupied with the next quota to hit or the next deadline to meet, and they aren't emotionally or even mentally available to their wives and children. Again, don't get me wrong; I don't feel that any of these desires of "success" are all that bad in and of themselves, but I don't feel that trading a healthy marriage or a relationship with your kids is worth it.

What I'd like to do is influence a third type of man—the ultimate family man. Am I personally there yet? I don't think so, but I do work tirelessly every single day to move closer to this reality. The type of man that I'd like to influence and inspire lives for his family. He isn't willing to settle for either providing for them financially by working 80-100 hours per week, or just being there physically, but having no motivation or inspiration to provide more than just getting by. My dream is to awaken in men the desire to live lives of priority, not obligation. This would be a life in which they can provide a secure financial future for their family but do so on their own terms. This would be a life in which they can build a business of their own, but do it in a way that the income is systematized.

This is what attracted me to network marketing because I met people in this industry that had those types of results. My first mentors in network marketing were living my definition of success. They have a wonderful faith life, a large home on a very private, exclusive lake, and they have a wonderful marriage as well as relationships with their friends and teammates. They lead by example and take responsibility for failures in their lives. One member of this couple has been free of his engineering job for well over a decade. To me, they were an example for me to follow and they personified my definition of success. There was just one BIG problem...they built their organization in the early 2000's in an offline fashion, and I came into the industry in 2010.

The internet and social media were changing the profession right under our noses, but I was still being taught outdated strategies, which did not help me build the same types of results that they did. The result was I got personal results early in my network marketing journey because I earned the respect of people in my market and they joined me in business. Many of them fell away over time because they weren't willing to "pay the price" and do what it took to build a business in network marketing offline: endless home and hotel meetings, one on ones, out of town seminars and national conventions. The pain of change was greater than the pain of staying the same, so they went back to the lives in which they were comfortable. Their dream wasn't big enough. I struggled for the next six years in my network marketing journey because my dream was big enough, but I was getting more and more frustrated with my lack of results due to outdated strategies and tactics. It wasn't until a cold winter day in 2016 when my business took a major turn for the better, and I found my "missing link."

My wife had run into the grocery store after church on a bright, sunny, and very crisp December Sunday. I pulled out my cell phone and started flipping through my Facebook newsfeed to pass the time. What I saw next has changed our lives and is the reason we are where we are today in business. I read a post that talked about a stay-at-home mom who built an organization of over 8,300 customers and distributors, earning a multiple six-figure income, and she did so entirely through prospecting and recruiting through Facebook from home! She was a mom to two high energy boys and wanted to be present in her home and available for her children and her husband, and she was tired of running around town doing meetings in coffee shops all the time. Long story short, I clicked on what I found out to be an advertisement for a mentorship company that specializes in teaching network marketers how to transition their business building skill sets from offline strategies and tactics to online strategies and tactics through informational products and mentorship from six, seven and eight-figure earners in the internet marketing space.

I dove head first into mentorship and haven't picked my head up for the last 16 months! In my mind, THIS was the information I was missing. This was the reason why I was stuck and struggling. I was sold a HOME business, but after working my 9-5, choking down a quick dinner, and kissing my wife and kids goodbye again to do a meeting, I was never present in the home. And if I was in the home, I was mentally and emotionally somewhere else, lost in the business frustrations as well as the financial stresses. What I saw in that Facebook ad was my chance at freedom and success, which was to be debt and financially free and have the time to spend with my wife and kids.

When I got started online, I didn't even recognize that what I was looking at was an advertisement until I got to a sales page. I was clueless to the fact that there were people out there building sales funnels, which were running largely on autopilot, and were generating leads and sales for people, including network marketers! I was also amazed and a bit angry to learn that the key to building a business that will last long after you're gone is to build a personal brand. I was never taught this! It's not about branding your company and spamming your company logo and latest incentives all over your Facebook wall, in order to "advertise." It is also not about sending copy-and-paste messages to people that you just "friended" in an attempt to get them to ask you what you do, and then prospect them for your business. It is about becoming an expert in the field who demonstrates leadership by having a vision for their lives and their teams, building influence by providing value into the marketplace consistently, building "know, like and trust" with their tribe, and developing a soft heart for people. That means loving them where they are, but at the same time having a thick skin to be able to handle the haters and the naysayers. What

I've learned over the last 16 months is that it is possible to prospect and recruit largely on autopilot, leveraging social media platforms and the internet to get your marketing message out to very specific, targeted people in the world. In network marketing, not everyone is your prospect. The "3-foot rule" is garbage. The skill sets to learn, in my opinion, in 21st century network marketing are getting comfortable going live on a Facebook live video, learning copywriting skills to develop a marketing message through Facebook ads, blog posts, and emails that are captivating, influencing, and entertaining, and learning some of the technical skills that it takes to build an online sales funnel. This way, when you are talking to a prospect online using a video chat such as zoom, they are 1. targeted, 2. qualified, and 3. already interested in your product, service, or opportunity. Say goodbye to having to overcome the pyramid objection!

Since beginning to learn these skill sets, from scratch with zero online or technical experience (remember I'm a physical therapist for crying out loud), I have been able to achieve some pretty cool results. I built a Facebook fan page from zero to over 7,000 targeted fans, built an email list of over 1,100 targeted subscribers, and generated five figures of additional revenue into my business within the first six months of learning these skill sets.

I even got my website/blog set up and started generating leads and sales on nearly a daily basis! Now I don't say this to brag, but to inspire those who are reading this chapter to know that you, too, can get these results. It just takes persistence, grit, and a willingness to learn some new skill sets. These skill sets will be valuable to learn because once you master them, you can literally print money. What I mean by that is that you'll know how to generate customers and sales on autopilot with leverage in any niche or business you want in the future! How exciting is that? You just have to get a big enough dream/target, learn some stuff, and get to work! I have recently been asked to become a mentor to incoming students in the same company that I got started mentoring with 16 months ago. How cool is that? The information works and is valuable if it can propel a no-tech physical therapist from no results online to becoming a leader and expert in online network marketing in 16 months!

I'd like to conclude with this thought for you. I hesitated to write about my results because I didn't want to come off as bragging. I know I don't have it all figured out, and I'm nowhere near the results that I'm looking for in my life or my business career. However, the path is clear. I have focus, direction, mentors, and a strategy that flat out works. And the end result will provide my definition of success, which is to be able to live a life of my priorities, not my obligations. I'm never going to "haveta." And, you don't "haveta" either. If you have a target, are willing to learn some skill sets, are willing to mentor and grow into your leadership potential, you too can design your ideal life. That can be the kind of life from which you don't have to take a vacation. That can be the kind of lifestyle that was probably promoted to you when you got started in network marketing or business in general in the first place. It's time to move into 21st-century business, and the internet and social media are already playing a massive role. Are you ready to skill up and lead your family? I hope you are. I'm in your corner, and I'm cheering you on to your victory and your personal definition of success.

Biography

Dr. Jim Storhok is a 21st Century Network Marketer who specializes in coaching and training other network marketers to utilize the internet, especially social media, to create automated leads and sales for their business. His passions include spending both quality and quantity time with his wife and children, improving the professionalism of network marketing through improved processes and systems, and inspiring other men to live lives of priority, not just obligation.

Contact Information

Facebook https://www.facebook.com/DrJimStorhokpage/
LinkedIn https://www.linkedin.com/in/drjimstorhok/
Twitter https://twitter.com/DrStorhok
Instagram https://www.instagram.com/drjimstorhok/
Website http://drjimstorhok.com/

Chapter 5

KEY TO SUCCESS IS FOCUS

By Jason Reid

"Success is finding within yourself the ability to leave everyday, thing, and person better than you found them. And be happy doing it." - Jason Reid

I remember being all scrunched up over an actual non-electronic tablet, the old paper kind, with a pencil, writing the table of contents for my new "bestseller." I was probably about eleven years of age. I'm pretty sure it got thrown out a few years later, and I can't remember if I ever did get past the first chapter or not. Next was a string of businesses ranging from collecting worms in the yard to sell for bait, to making bow and arrows, to canoes, to looking for a newspaper route, to building hang gliders. None of them, including the last, ever "got off the ground." I still can't quite put my finger on exactly what it was that put such an entrepreneurial drive into me, perhaps partly being the oldest in the family, or being homeschooled, giving me a personal sense of independence.

The seed of that desire I consider a gift of "grace." It seems to me that those who have that seed know it, it might be small, but it's still there. And some of the tiniest seeds grow into the largest trees. So, for me, the question was how to cultivate that seed, so it becomes a tree of success. The answers eluded me for years, and it seemed life was against me. Everything I tried went sour. One venture to the next, from my late teens into mid-twenties, and all these great ideas (or so I thought!) would stay just out of my grasp. I, among others in my social group, was often heard saying on numerous occasions "a day late and a dollar short" of the opportunities that would seemingly slip through our fingers. "The rich get richer, and the poor get poorer" was our motto, insinuating that we were on the "poor" end of the spectrum.

In the end, I got a job, which was a good thing. I am in full agreement with Robert Kiyosaki in "Rich Dad, Poor Dad," the best reason for having a job is to gain a real-world education.

There are lessons to be learned that can be best learned as an employee. First "real" job was as a carpenter building houses. From there, to a sales position at a building materials supplier. After four years, it was time to move on, and being married with two children by this time made it a serious venture, but the desire for something more won out, and we relocated. With the move came the start of yet a new business as an independent building contractor, this time, somewhat successful due to having learned a trade and determination. It wasn't easy, but we got by. Barely.

Fast forward a few years, and that brings us to the recession of 2008, a turning point in the lives of many. Work just dried up to virtually nothing, and it was a tough time in more ways than just financially. During this time, I also met a few key people who were very influential on my thinking, perhaps most importantly in helping me change my view of myself. This combined with the need to do something different to support a family, and the dream of doing more while still alive created a breakthrough for me. It wasn't a huge, radical, change-everything-in-an-instant kind, but a major deciding point that something HAD to change. And the catalyst for bringing that change about for me was FOCUS. Not in the sense of blindly seeing only one thing to the detriment of everything else, but a discipline of mind to not lose sight of the goal. In business, it can be easy to be driven, and forget the other aspects of life. Like being a husband and father, or a friend. So, the focus needs to be on the several aspects of ONE whole. My focus looks like this: Personal development, Relationships, Business. And yes, in that order. I look at this as three sides of ONE triangle.

When discussing focus, usually someone will inevitably mention the fact that you can only ride one horse at a time, a statement I fully agree with, but you do have to take care of multiple aspects of that horse to get anywhere. One must pay attention to what reins you are pulling on, watch for possible obstacles in the path, and stay on the horse all at the same time. You could concentrate only on staying on the horse and successfully do so, but you might get a surprise where you end up! And I think this way of looking at it was the key to unlocking the power of focus for me.

We all know someone who focused very well, but all they focused on was money. Focusing on that single aspect is just like staying on the horse. If that is what they truly wanted, be it far from me to state otherwise, but for most people, I think that gets them somewhere they probably didn't want to go. So as you can see, I have a definite, focused idea of what "focus" means! Though to illustrate what it has done for me, I am going to "focus" on only one side of the triangle- the business.

At the turning point, there was a decision to make. In my field of interest, there was only one way that made sense to move forward with, to make my mark. And that was the quality of craftsmanship. I focused on that product, looking for that particular, yet elusive, level of excellence I wanted. Practically speaking, this was not a pretty sight. It ended up being years of many late nights into the early hours of the morning. Thousands of dollars "wasted" in materials, listening to criticism from experts, and discovering good ideas that weren't. And yet, through it, all progress was made. Not overnight, but slowly my skill improved. I had a coach that made a tremendous difference. He couldn't do what I was doing to save his life but had the ability to help me see myself and my work from another point of view. It was a priceless experience.

Through all this was the key of focus, remaking the decision by the hour if necessary, to not take my eyes off the goal and the vision. I could see what I wanted to create in my mind, and I had to concentrate on it. Not a visualization process that brought magical results, but to not allow that image of who I wanted to be, a master in my field, fade into the background, pressured out by the noise of life. Yes, take care of what needs to be taken care of. If your mother is in the hospital, go and visit her. Maybe even if she's not. But never let the vision fade, DO something every day to bring you closer to your dream. That, to me, is focus. It's living life on purpose. Reminds me of one of Tony Robbin's great quotes,

"One reason so few of us achieve what we truly want is that we never direct our focus, we never concentrate our power. Most people dabble their way through life, never deciding to master anything in particular." - Tony Robbins.

An element of focus that was a challenge for me was to keep it positive. I remember many times, sitting there immediately after making a fatal mistake in a matter of seconds that destroyed hours of careful work. In those moments, the destiny was decided, keeping focused on the vision I wanted to achieve. And even repeating to myself over and over like a mantra, "I can do this, I can do this, I can do this." Then taking several deep breaths before starting over again. It happens by doing whatever it takes to maintain the focus like your life depends on it. Because it does. And this would be especially difficult for those whose close family members and loved ones are NOT supportive of their dream.

And it worked! People began asking for my product. The icons of my field began asking my opinions. I was offered contracts. Something was changing. I had another job to make ends meet by this time in the story. Financially, life was satisfactory. But life can be interesting sometimes, and circumstances came together to help keep me focused, pressure from behind and pull from the front you might say. It was time to make another decision and use what I had learned and move to the next level. Applying the lessons I had learned, and not stopping, has propelled me to the next level. I quit my job and went into business full-time, a daring move for anyone. The focus did not let me down, and today, I am a respected leader in my field, the business is thriving, the future looks bright, and we are just getting started.

The satisfaction of success is immense, and it would be my wish that everyone could experience it. Experiencing success is a life-changing event, once tasted, you can never live without it again. The beauty of it is that life is a journey and the opportunity to continually experience success is part of that journey, not a goal in the end. True success can actually start the first day a decision is made. I will admit it was hard to feel it then, but looking back, I can see it. I am no different than anyone else; I'm not any more special than anyone else. But the power of a decision, especially the one to live by, a different mindset than before, can separate someone from the rest of the crowd.

I am definitely not done with this success thing, and I think the ultimate success is to help other people to find it. To be the catalyst in someone's life that propels them to the next level. Now, wouldn't THAT be something satisfying to focus on?

Biography

Jason Reid is a self-made entrepreneur who has built several successful businesses. He currently owns and operates Hawkeye Falconry Supply, suppliers of The Finest Falconry Furniture, where all products are handcrafted to the highest specifications. He values the skills involved in his specialized field and the unique responsibilities involved in working with birds-of-prey which provides a basis for the qualities needed to be successful in any endeavor.

He has a passion for using these virtues to help others in areas of personal development, finance, and charitable work.

He has been published in American Falconry magazine and was a past columnist for "Feathers and Friends" children's magazine.

His accomplishments include a falcon breeding project that helped with the reintroduction of the once-endangered birds, and he continues to be involved in conservation projects and wild bird rehabilitation efforts.

He is a member of the North American Falconers Association, International Eagle Austringer Association, Indiana Falconers Association, and various other state and regional conservation and educational organizations. He enjoys several outdoor sports including camping and boating, as well as spending time with his family and birds. He currently resides in Fort Wayne Indiana with his wife and four children.

Contact Information

Facebook https://www.facebook.com/JasonReidHawkeye
LinkedIn https://www.linkedin.com/in/jason-reid-a054b7166

CHAPTER 6

ROADBLOCKS IN LIFE COME FROM OUR MINDSET

By Robert Bucko

I was born in 1984 in a small town called Snina in the eastern part of Slovakia, which is one of the poorest areas of my country. My parents worked hard to get my brother and me to University. Their mindset (and many other people's during the time) was to go to school, get the best grades, get to University, get a "stable" job (meaning they cannot fire you) to get a "secure" income. The reason my parents taught me to get a University degree and a well-paying job was because of my health conditions. My parents were always giving me all the support I needed over time. Even when I did not realize it, they were still there for me, and I am exceedingly thankful for my family. When I was a year old, doctors diagnosed me with a joint disease called "Magnus Perthes," which means my hip joints are not developed, and I will walk in pain. So when I was two years old, I was sent to a clinic for 14 months where it was forbidden for me to walk.

After the time in the clinic, I had to learn how to walk again. When I was ten years old, I had an operation where the doctors had to break my right hip joint, turn it around and fix it with a steel plate and four screws for it to heal. I remember the Head of the orthopedic department saying, "We will have to replace your joint for a titanium one by the time you are 25 years old." I lived with that statement for a long time.

I could not play any sports for my entire childhood. That is my background, and all those aspects shaped my life. I was one of the best students at school and got into University, where I studied programming and information technologies, which is one of the best-paying professions, even today.

I was also doing research in the field of applied informatics during my Ph.D. studies and also made some professional publications on the topic. I got so many great deals and job offers, but somehow, I knew that it would not fulfill my calling. I wanted to discover how I can use my skills and my expertise to serve others better. That was when I started my first company, before I even finished my university studies. It was a language school where we taught people new languages to get better jobs, positions or even start a new career abroad. Education was always the key element in my life, but very soon I realized formal education is not enough. I needed to get new skills to help more people faster, better and more efficiently.

When I was 28 years old, I was expecting to go in for the surgery to replace my hip joint for the titanium one. When I came for the last checkup, the doctor told me that I did not need the replacement, and I can come in for the next checkup only if I have some pain in my legs. I will be 34 this year, and I feel completely well. I also run and play sports on a daily basis without limitations.

You can read my story "How I was healed by God" on my blog www.robertbucko.com/blog.

After some time, I realized that all the roadblocks experienced in life come from our mindset.

I graduated from one of the most difficult Universities in my country, but that did not give me what I was expecting. The opportunity to go further with an education came with my education company. I am not saying that a University degree is not valuable, it was valuable in my case. I just want to emphasize the power of personal growth.

I have invested thousands of Euros into my own personal training. I realize that growth happens only if you are <u>constantly</u> learning. Persistence is the key to overcome any roadblocks.

People in my country still value a University education very highly. I was taught that the only way to success is to work hard for 12-16 hours a day and work for "someone" else. It all depends on who you know and if you have good connections in the right places. And because we still have such thinking, University education is still a big deal in my country.

My goal is to reprogram such thinking and teach people to reclaim responsibility from "the government, the boss, wife, husband, kids, young age, old age, etc." That is why I started an education program for young people called "Program Leader." In this program, we teach students the English language, as English opens up doors to the world, and also personal development strategies, techniques, and methods of how they can change their thinking, how to become a leader in their community, how to work on your dreams, and overcome fears that limit us.

One of my great role models taught me to build up the value of your mind. That means, no matter what the circumstances are, try to increase the value of your mind. Anything might happen to you as a person, or to your business, your career, your partnership, but no one can take away what you have learned, no one can delete your expertise, the unique perspective you have obtained from your experiences. That is the value you can bring to others, or in other words, to serve others.

My life taught me to be grateful for every minute you have in this life. I am so thankful for what God has done in my life. It is not possible to describe it in words, I am thankful for my wife, and I have just become a daddy last week of two beautiful princesses. We are full of joy, appreciation, gratefulness, and blessings. It changed the game in my life. I encourage you to stay on your track and lead yourself as the captain of the boat.

But it does not happen overnight. The single most important key to achieving success is to know crystal clear what "SUCCESS" means to YOU and then make a roadmap on how to get there. The amazing thing about that road is the never-ending process. When you get to the TOP, you will get another perspective that excites you even more.

I believe there are proven ways on how to achieve anything in your life. It requires a certain level of leadership. My first lesson on leadership was to learn how to lead myself. If you master that, you are 80% done. I would love to share my strategies and tools on how I get better every day and what keeps me on track to constantly give my better self to the world.

There are 2 KEY QUESTIONS to make your dreams come alive.

1. Knowing where I am
2. Knowing where I want to go, which includes knowing what I want to do and also knowing who I want to be (this one is the most important). Let's take a closer look at what I mean by these keys.

1. Knowing where I am. I make sure to have a good mirror. It is essential to know where I am in life, with my finances, with my relationships, with my health, and wealth as it applies to all the other areas of life. I discovered that for many people it is difficult

to answer this question, "Where are you at the moment?" I do not mean physically, but where are you as a human being, as a person in terms of fulfilling your calling? Some great questions helped me understand where I was in my own life and it was a great impulse to establish new goals and habits that helped me to reach what I wanted with less stress, less time, and fewer resources.

Try this exercise. Complete the sentences below. Write down the first thing that comes to your mind.

Life is…
Success is…
Love is…
Passion is…
Happiness is…
Joy is…
The reasons WHY I am/I am NOT/successful are…
The reasons WHY I am/I am NOT/happy are…
My biggest fears are…
The most beautiful thing about my life is…
The worst thing in my life is…

These questions give you a significant reflection, which could lead to starting a change (or a small shift) you need to do, or you are about to do. I answer them from time to time to make my vision clear. If you are honest with yourself, it is a great reflection and amazing tool to start something new or improve the way you are currently on. The great thing about this is that even if you answered these questions yesterday, today is a new day and you are not the same as you were yesterday. So much is happening in our everyday life, we learn, we reach, we love, we discover, we develop, and so on. This exercise is never the same, and it gives you the reflection of where you are at the moment.

2. Knowing/discovering:

a) where I want to go:

I always make sure to write down all of my goals. There are three stages in writing my goals list. I will not go into details on how to visualize or write down your specific goal using any well-known strategy (S.M.A.R.T. goals etc.), but I will explain the process of making such a list and how it will influence your mindset and decision making.

The First stage is: I write down all the goals which occupied my mind the most, therefore most of them are "urgent goals" such as: repair the roof, get a bigger car for my two kids where you can put a pushchair and suitcase in as well, change the flat for a bigger one, and the list continues... Interesting things happen when you do not STOP writing your goals and finish your list of urgent goals.

The second stage starts right after you will start thinking about the things you want to do, you want to achieve, you desire or dream about. Examples: go for a 2-month vacation with your family, travel around the world, see the most amazing places, buy the most amazing car, move to a better place, and so on. You will start changing things for experiences or improvements to your lifestyle! Something that will create amazing memories that you are able to collect and enjoy.

The third stage is about WHO you want to become, who you want to meet with, what significant project you want to work on, how you want to improve other people's lives, etc. One of the exercises I would recommend is to write down 101 goals. Why 101? First of all, it is more than 100. If you tell yourself to write down 100 goals, most people will end up with 60, 70 or 80; they will barely reach 90. When you tell yourself to write down 101, it is a specific number, so you will go through the process of all the stages just as described above, that is WHY 101. Writing those goals will be challenging, but make sure you enjoy the entire process, it is not a race, you have the time, and it is one of the biggest investments you could give yourself.

b) what I want to do

This question opens up the "HOW" method. How are you going to fulfill your calling? What strategy or method do you have to follow to get the results you want. There is one very simple, but useful farmer proverb in my country.

"If you want to have the same harvest as the best farmer in your village, go and ask him how he did it. Then just follow his instructions."

There are many great and proven strategies and business models in today's world to follow. There are so many great leaders in a particular industry who you can follow and use the same strategies, methods or instruction to get the results you want. That is why I want to partner with Matt Morris. I think he is a great leader with extraordinary results. I am super excited to be a co-author with Matt and learn those strategies from the TOP leaders in the industry. As the proverb said: "Just follow the instructions."

c) Who I want to be (this one is the most important)

We have been created by the Creator in His image, that means: we are called to CREATE as well. That is why we, as human beings, are called creatures (creatures = those who create). It is that simple. How would you feel if you could create anything with no limits? Just imagine that. Make a clear picture in your mind of how exactly your life would look like if you had the power to create anything? How would you feel if you knew your specific calling, your purpose, why you have been installed into the current space and time? I can tell you there is no OTHER person exactly the same as YOU! Never was and never will be. You are UNIQUE, and this uniqueness is the way you see things in the world, in other people, your experiences, skills, and background are so valuable that someone is willing to pay a high price to get to know your view, your advice, and your point. The truth is, you have the power. Just STEP UP and BE who you are called to be! If you know who you are and the price of yourself, you become unstoppable.

These areas are essential to understanding who we are, why we are here, and what we are called to do. If you are not clear in any of those questions, it will make you go around searching and looking for new opportunities, new doors to open, from one training to another and so on. On the other hand, if you have a crystal-clear vision of those areas, you will make decisions or take actions, and it will get you to the mode of certainty, and you will be aware of the value you carry or present.

I used these exact strategies to build my companies. I made exact plans to achieve them. And you can too!

Biography

Robert Bucko found his passion for serving others. He helps people find their talents and strengths. He is the co-founder of the Institute of Education that provides leadership programs for people to change their mindset from fear to courage and victory.

Contact Information

Facebook: https://www.facebook.com/robert.bucko.9
LinkedIn: https://www.linkedin.com/in/robertbucko/

YouTube
Channel: https://www.youtube.com/channel/UCaYHj1mABKAh
FG4cYF9cpew?view_as=subscriber
Twitter: @BuckoRobert
Instagram: https://www.instagram.com/robertbucko/
Website: https://www.robertbucko.com/
Blog: https://www.robertbucko.com/blog

Chapter 7

HOW I WENT THROUGH THE LOWEST OF LOWS TO BECOME SUCCESSFUL

By Jamie Lester

Even though I was raised in what would be considered a white-collar family, the value and ethics of hard work were drummed into me from a young age, and my father wasted no time in teaching me the value of a dollar.

From the age of thirteen, I would spend every vacation working in my family business which was never a chore because I was always passionate about the business. We lived in Martinsville, VA and my family owned a company that produced building components for the housing industry. I always knew that after I finished college, I would join the family business.

I graduated from Virginia Tech in 1986, and a few years later my father's health started to decline. As a family, we decided that the best option would be to sell the business. I was 25 years old at the time, and for the first time in my life, I had no idea about my future.

I went back to business school at Wake Forest University, and after I graduated I took a job at a certified public accountant (CPA) firm, formerly Coopers & Lybrand; now PricewaterhouseCoopers.

During my time there, I worked with a variety of different businesses that were facing bankruptcy, which equipped me with the skill set and confidence to buy back my family business when it began to struggle financially. I originally had a partner who was an investment banker, but the partnership did not work out. We both wanted very different things. My long-term plan was to restore the business to the way it once was whereas my partner wanted to sell off the assets and then close the business down. I ended up buying him out only to discover that the business was in far worse condition than I initially thought.

I had to invest all the money I had at the time into the business, and for about ten years things were going very well; however, everything changed in 2008 when the mortgage crisis hit. We could not weather the storm this time around, and I ended up having to file for both corporate and personal bankruptcy. I lost everything except my retirement accounts. Other than losing my mother, it was the lowest point of my life. For me, having money and losing it was worse than never having it at all.

After the business went under, I moved to Charleston, South Carolina to start afresh. Things started to change when I spoke with my 72-year old cousin who had been in the real estate business for some time. He had lost everything and rebuilt it several times. He told me, "If you haven't gone broke at least once in your life, you don't have any lead in your pencil," and that I could make more money but I could not make more time. The advice he gave me made me realize that as long as time was on my side, there would always be opportunities to make more money and I took that to heart.

The one thing that I was sure of was going on someone's payroll wasn't an option. I was prepared to work as hard as I needed to, but I wanted the reward to be mine and no one else's. I founded my present business in 2011, and since then I have never looked back.

If my new business has taught me anything, it is that you will only be truly successful if you are completely passionate about what you do, and you put your heart in it. If you do not believe in yourself and the value that your business offers, then others are not going to believe in you either.

Another key to success is that you have to be a great leader. You may not think that this is something which is inside you, but I believe that it is something which is in everybody. If you do not have good leadership, then it does not matter how good the rest of your business is. Only good leadership will bring real success.

I believe that there are eight key steps to becoming a great leader.

#1 Planning

You need to focus on the things that are the most important and be decisive when it is needed most.

The true champions have a plan, commit to the plan, and then establish a routine to execute that plan. Ramon Floyd, past champion of the Masters Golf Tournament, was interviewed about his preparation for that tournament because of the uniqueness of the golf course. He said months before the tournament he would write down his strategy and the way he was going to play every shot on all 18 holes. What he found out was whenever he had a bad shot or had a bad hole, he was able to jump right back into his game plan and not waste another shot or hole. He had committed to it, so when something went wrong, he was ready. He said preparation and committing to his plan was everything.

#2 Motivation and Passion

You need motivation and desire. This is what is going to carry you through the days when things get tough.

Maintain a positive attitude and enthusiasm. Charles Swindoll said, "The longer I live, the more I realize the impact of attitude on life. Attitude to me is more important than facts, more important than the past, more important than education, money, circumstances, more important than failures, successes, what other people think or say or do. More important than giftedness or skill. It will make or break a company."

#3 Hard Work

You are always prepared to put in the hard work to get things done. I believe you can beat 50% of the competition just by showing up, another 40% by doing what's right which is looking people in the eye and being honest, and that last 10% is a dogfight, having desire, loving what you're doing, rolling out of bed with a blueprint and ready to go after it.

#4 Passion

If you're going to be effective, you have to set yourself on fire. You must do something, get uncomfortable, and work like you have never worked before for a good amount of time. You have to create a fire in your organization, and it's hard to do that if you haven't first created a passion inside yourself.

#5 Be a Good Listener

Sometimes, people on the ground know a lot more about the business than you do. It's okay to acknowledge the fact that a leader does not need to know everything. He can take the counsel of wise and able people.

#6 Hire people smarter than you

When two people agree on everything, one of them is unnecessary. Surround yourself with great people with a vision who are ready to fight for their success and do it positively; people who are tired of sitting on the sidelines and are ready to go out and make their mark.

#7 Know the ins and outs of your business

Be a student of your business. Know your subject. Leaders don't go to sleep at the wheel. They know everything that is going on in their business.

#8 Know when things are not working

Recognize when things are not working and be ready to change course.

If you know it is going to hurt when you don't meet your goals, you will work extra hard to achieve them. It is okay to take failure personally because this is what is going to spur you on to do better the next time.

Your attitude is also going to play a large part in your success. When you wake up each morning, you do not know what challenges you are going to face. However, what you do know is that you will be facing these challenges with a positive attitude and this is half the battle.

Successful people have fear just like all of us. But they do things in spite of the fear. I believe that fear should not stop you from achieving your goals. You should take fear head on and do things that you fear the most. Tom Cruise in the movie Days of Thunder says, "I am more afraid of being nothing than I am of being hurt." That's how I've lived my life.

Closing Thoughts

To be successful in business, you must be willing to go through the dump, just don't hang out there. Losing and not accomplishing your goals must hurt and be so offensive to you that you are not going to accept it. We have a choice every day regarding the attitude we will embrace for that day. We cannot change our past; we cannot change the fact that people will act the way they want. We cannot change the inevitable. The only thing we can do is play on the one string that we have, and that's our attitude. Life is 5% of what happens to us and 95% of how we react to it. We are in charge of our attitudes. Sometimes you have to go through the absolute worst to get to the best times of your life.

Biography

Jamie Lester has a B.S. in Marketing and Finance from Virginia Tech, and an MBA from Wake Forest University. Whether he's interviewing someone to join his business or sitting with a client, he is always looking to uncover their pain and find a solution. He takes a hands-on approach to solving problems by getting down in the trenches with people rather than sitting in an ivory tower.

Contact Information

Facebook: https://www.facebook.com/The-Lester-Agency-873623722798474/
Twitter: https://twitter.com/Officelesterag1
Instagram: https://www.instagram.com/office132/
LinkedIn: https://www.linkedin.com/in/lester-agency-344105160/

Chapter 8

FEAR AND SELF-DOUBT TO FEELING GOOD IN MY OWN BODY

By Adda Hafborg

"The more we hide our feelings, the more they show. The more we deny our feelings, the more they grow." - Unknown

Here is a gift from me to you. My story can hopefully help someone in the journey from fear and self-doubt to feeling good in their own body and mind. I lived a good, safe life in Iceland with my hubby, my teenage daughter and our three dogs in a beautiful modern house with two cars. Both of us had good jobs.

But, I have always known that I am not an ordinary woman who is satisfied with living life without action and adventure. I didn't want to listen to my inner self for many years, because from the outside, everything looked good and I felt okay. But, something was missing in my life.

Deep down in my heart, I desired more freedom to travel the world, learn about other countries and get to know more people and their cultures. One cold day in November 2011, our friends came over, and they wanted us to work with them on network marketing.

For three years, people all around me had tried to recruit me into this "thing," but I had tried network marketing twice in the past, and I was never going to do it again. The strange thing is that whenever I say to myself "never again," the opposite seems to happen. I am very polite, so I said "yes" when they showed us the presentation, but after that, I said a BIG "NO, THANK YOU." When they were leaving, one of our friends said these golden words to me "Adda, it is ok to change your mind." That night, I could not sleep; my mind was on fire.

"This is good; this is something for me, I can do this." After three days, I called one of our friends and asked, "Can you guys sign me in, please?" After one year of all kinds of struggles and victories, I decided to go all in, and I quit my corporate job. People around me were skeptical and asked, "Are you really going to quit a very good job for this pyramid thing?" I said 'yes' with pride, but deep inside, I was scared. "What if this is not going to work for me?" My fear and self-doubt started to kick in, but with positive self-talk and reading books about personal development, I kept on going. My hubby and I made a contract with each other before quitting my job. If my salary in our network marketing company did not at least double in six months, I would look for another job. I was unstoppable. I did not want to look for another job. I loved the people and the freedom in network marketing.

I had made my decision... My eyes glowed with positive energy. "Let's do this," I said. My mind was full of faith; I believed in myself, the company and my team. The growth started to be unbelievably fantastic. For two and a half years, we had great MOMENTUM, and we started to build businesses in other countries as well.

The internet is a great tool to build businesses worldwide. My team was growing fast. I started to travel the world to support my team, and I loved it. I am so grateful for all the great friendships I have built with fantastic people all over the world because of network marketing. I have friends in Iceland, Holland, Michigan, Minnesota, Denmark, Norway, Sweden, Finland, Spain, Germany, Latvia, Estonia and many more.

Then during the summer of 2015, life happened to me. I had self-doubt to the point that I was making my decisions based on what other people were saying about me behind my back, not what I knew was the truth about myself. I was constantly struggling with confidence and always second-guessing myself. What I've learned from my experiences is that I need to feed my mind with positivity every single day. I need to surround myself with positive people who think of solutions like me.

All of us have good and bad days in our lives. I truly believe that if I let go of other people's opinions and listen to my own positive voice every single day, I can find a positive daily balance. I've found out a few things that help a lot with my self-doubt and confidence; these may help you too:

1. Stop comparing my accomplishments to that of my friends and colleagues.

I find that I doubt myself the most when I'm comparing what I'm doing with what other people are doing. When I compare my accomplishments to a colleague, I start feeling inadequate. My colleague's accomplishments are not a litmus test for my success. One key thing to remember when we find ourselves in this mental pattern is that everyone is on his or her own journey. I find that I am most successful in my personal and professional life when I am following what works for me and what makes me feel good, even if it is different from what the people I look up to are doing.

2. Forget about what everyone is thinking about me.

When we care about what everyone else is thinking about us, we inhibit ourselves. We often would rather do nothing and not get judged than do something and risk being criticized. Worrying about what other people think of us will continue to hold us back from doing some great things.

3. Accept that my fears and doubts are within me, and I need to give them room, and not try to escape them.

Whatever thoughts and feelings come up inside of me, I'll be ok with them. Stop resisting what I feel and think. Avoidance is not the answer. Even though fear and doubt are painful, they are not the problem; my reaction to them is. Problems arise when we try to get rid of, hide or control our self-doubt and fear. When we start accepting how we feel and think in any given moment, we start noticing that feelings and thoughts are like the clouds in the sky; they are just passing by.

Whenever I feel the urge not to take action, I remind myself to act on what I truly desire: making meaningful connections and enjoying life to the fullest.

4. I believe pure gratitude from our hearts is a powerful help in every situation in our lives.

In a study by McCraty and colleagues (1998), 45 adults were taught to "cultivate appreciation and other positive emotions." The results of this study showed that there was a mean 23% reduction in the stress hormone cortisol after the intervention period.

Moreover, during the use of the techniques, 80% of the participants exhibited an increased coherence in heart rate variability patterns, indicating reduced stress. In other words, these findings suggest that people with an "attitude of gratitude" experience lower levels of stress.

In another study by Seligman, Steen, and Peterson (2005), participants were given one week to write and then deliver a letter of thanks in person to someone who had been especially kind to them, but who had never been properly thanked.

The gratitude visit involves three basic steps:

First, think of someone who has done something important and wonderful for you, yet who you feel you have not properly thanked.

Next, reflect on the benefits you received from this person, and write a letter, expressing your gratitude for all they have done for you.

Finally, arrange to deliver the letter personally, and spend some time with this person talking about what you wrote.

The results showed that participants who engaged in the letter-writing exercise reported more happiness for one month after the intervention compared to a control group. Expressing gratitude not only helps us to appreciate what we received in life; it also helps us to feel that we've given something back to those who helped us.

5. Read positive books every day.

One of the best ways to boost my confidence is to listen to or read some of my favorite self-development books.

My favorite sources are:
- The Magic Of Thinking Big by David J. Schwartz
- The Greatest Networker In The World by John M. Fogg
- The Seasons Of Life by Jim Rohn
- Think And Grow Rich by Napoleon Hill

I put the audiobooks on my iPhone and listen to them whenever I'm walking, driving or chilling at the beach. I also spend quiet time on my balcony with a book.

6. Write in a gratitude journal at the beginning of each day.

It is so easy to focus on what we don't have rather than what we do have. Giving those feelings energy will only create more situations which I don't like to have in my life.

Instead of focusing on what I am lacking, I like to focus on what I have and what I have accomplished. Feelings of gratitude put us in a positive frame of mind. When we're feeling positive, we're feeling good. And when we're feeling good, good things happen.

7. When my decisions were made back then, I had many negative thoughts, my self-doubt took over, and I often gave up even before I started.

Mel Robbins' tips. "The 5-second rule," has changed my life. When I count 5-4-3-2-1 go... I just do the things I planned to do, and it feels good.

Okay, back to my story. All our five children had started their own lives; my husband and I were in our big house (with our dogs). That Fall of 2015, my hubby and I got divorced, and I moved out. I felt miserable. Few people knew that because I was always smiling, but in my eyes and in my heart, there was no joy. I kept on doing my network marketing business, but it was not easy. In one year, I lost about half of my team members. I was depressed and felt sorry for myself. "Poor, miserable me."

But one day, when the smell of the spring passed through my window, I decided that "Ok, Adda, now is the time for you to find your 'big girl shoes' and stop this negative nonsense." I remembered that somewhere in my notes, I had three great questions from the Dale Carnegie training that I had once used before at a difficult moment in my life.

Here are the three questions. It is very important to write down the answers honestly.
1. What is the worst thing that can happen?
2. What is the possible thing to do about it?
3. What am I going to do about it?

These questions helped me to focus on what I really want in life and to follow my dreams with a positive attitude. In July 2016, I decided to move to Spain. One of my best friends invited me to rent a room in her apartment near Torrevieja and see if I would like to build my own home in Spain one day.

It's been over two years now, and I am building up a fantastic life with my fiancé in a beautiful little town in southern Spain. I can go to Iceland to be with my grandchildren and my family, and they also come to Spain. The world is not so big after all. My network marketing business is growing again, and I am not scared of the future anymore.

It is up to me to accept my fear and self-doubt and put up a positive exception to every situation so that I can be the best version of myself on a daily basis. I believe that what we feed our brain daily is the foundation of our future. Hope you all are having a great day today, just like every other day.

Biography

Adda Hafborg is an Entrepreneur, Mentor, and Influencer. She has built her leaders' organization in 13 different countries. Her strength is her positive long-term vision. She influences others to reach their goals and find balance in life while she leads by example.

Contact Information

Facebook https://www.facebook.com/arny.halfdansdottir#!/arny.halfdansdottir
YouTube https://www.youtube.com/channel/UCeR16SV7vlekxEnbBMplwfw
Instagram https://www.instagram.com/addahafborg/

Chapter 9

WHAT MAKES SOME PEOPLE MORE SUCCESSFUL THAN OTHERS?

By Maxwell Adekoje

Why do some people do exceptionally well, and others don't? Every human being is built for success and wants to be successful, but only a few become successful. The percentage of successful people seems to be about 10 percent, about the same range, year after year.

What is success? How can you join this constant and unchanging 10% of the population?

Understanding success is the first step to attaining success. These principles took me from $20, when I first came to the US, to becoming a proud owner and CEO of an MLM marketing company.

Success is a thought process that gives birth to a discovered purpose. The most significant gap between successful and unsuccessful people is the way they think, which reflects on their attitude, beliefs, and mindset. If the way we think is paramount to our success, why do we still have the same wrong mindset? Let me share a little story I once heard from a friend.

In 1990, a known musician built a house with N20 Million; the same year, Jim Ovia started Zenith Bank with the same amount. Zenith bank in Nigeria is one of the most reputable banks in Africa.

Today, you and I don't have a room in the musician's house, but I have an account in Jim's bank, and you probably do, too.

The house was built in Lagos, Nigeria, and remains there to this date.

Jim's bank started in a corner and now has over 500 branches in Nigeria and many international branches.

Millions upon millions transact business in Jim's bank daily.

The house is becoming dilapidated. In 2015, he SPENT more money to renovate the house and bought a Nissan Pathfinder with

N10 million, an additional liability, while in the same 2015, Jim's bank MADE a profit of N105.7 billion.

Zenith bank employs hundreds of thousands of people and feeds families.

This is the difference between a successful mindset and an unsuccessful mindset. If you buy a car for N20 million today, in 20 years' time, you will be ashamed to drive it. On the other hand, if you invest that same amount in a lucrative business or an asset, it may be worth billions of nairas in 20 years. (Jim Ovia is now worth 980 million dollars, with the official dollar rate of N350. That means he is worth N313 BILLION NAIRA, all because of an investment of N20 million. Every penny in your hand is like a seed; you can decide to eat it or sow it. When you plant it, it will bear many more seeds in the future. Now, you can see why successful people think differently.

Success demands that you develop a certain type of thinking and perception about the way you see things. It doesn't matter how many degrees or talents you have; it's your thinking and attitude that keeps you small.

Attitude plays a vital ingredient in your success; it's a product of belief. You can't have an attitude beyond your belief. Your attitude comes from your platform of belief. If you associate with only poor individuals, you will think like them.

If you hang around the restaurant long enough, you will get something to eat. We become our environment unknowingly. Stay in an environment that will aid your growth.

People with a great attitude are coachable with a teachable and welcoming atmosphere. Take responsibility for your attitude; it belongs to you.

How can you alter your attitude? Here are three simple steps:
1. Fill your mind with good thinking; you can't fill your mind with bad stuff and expect to alter your mind. Be selective and guard your mind with armor.
2. Marinate and digest the good thinking you put in. Dr. Maxwell Maltz, a plastic surgeon turned psychologist, wrote: "It usually requires a minimum of about 21 days to effect any perceptible change in a mental image. Following plastic surgery, it takes about 21 days for the average patient to get used to his new face. When an arm or leg is amputated, the "phantom limb" persists for

about 21 days. People must live in a new house for about three weeks before it begins to "seem like a home."
3. Practice good things, so they get into your mind and become a part of you.

It's the thinking of a person that makes them see circumstances differently. After years of dealing with problems, I started realizing that a problem is a human definition of an opportunity to grow. If you call it a problem, it immediately takes a negative notation. If you see it as an opportunity, it becomes positive. A problem really only becomes a problem when you see it as a problem. If you want to become a person of impact, you must fill your mind correctly.

After reading the book, "Think & Grow Rich," repeatedly, I realize that human beings can alter their life by changing their attitude. Wow!

The most valuable instrument for success is the 15.24 cm between your ears. No one can live beyond the limit of their thinking; it must be altered. You're simply a presentation of your thoughts. Because of the way my mind was programmed as a child, I had to reprogram my thought process.

First, I had to discover my purpose in life, feed my mind with new beliefs. I'm possible. Marinate on the new thinking and back it up with execution.

Information does not bring transformation; conversion does.

If you don't like who you are, change it to who you think you should be. Your thinking is more powerful than any promise.

Everyone came to this earth fully loaded with purpose; discover it. You're important to the world with a purpose to do something significant. Most of our perceptions are other people's concept about us. You didn't know you were weak until someone told you. Your life is shaped and cultured by what you hear or see.

The little difference in people is their attitude; the larger version is if it is positive or negative.

A seed can be held in your wallet for 40 years and never become a tree even though the seed has a tree in it. Most people go through life carrying their greatness in their wallet rather than planting it.

Trees aren't found in the soil; they are hidden in the seed if you can get it out of your wallet and plant it.

We are like a tree serving the world our juice; plant yourself on fertile ground. Watch out for the weeds. People heading nowhere are ready to pollute your seed. Break away from people to become more. You must outgrow some people. I call it isolation. Know when to go! "Isolation to growth" is best illustrated by the story of a lobster. How do lobsters grow? A lobster is a soft animal that lives inside a rigid shell that never expands. So, how do they grow? By isolation.

A lobster isolates from predators and casts off the old shell and produces a new one; then, after a while, they repeat the process.

The lesson of the story: the lobster feels uncomfortable, then grows. Most people will never grow until they walk away from people who are continually polluting their life, solidifying the wrong beliefs in them.

Always walk away and remember to repeat this process of renewing your mind.

I can't end the chapter without talking about some key traits of success - confidence and focus.

Confidence

Confidence is a product of your belief. The way you think about yourself is the way you unknowingly behave. It's interesting how an elephant with so much power behaves like a gazelle in the presence of a lion.

Mindset

Mindset is everything; thinking is the belief system exposed. I had to alter my thinking, and my attraction instantly took a turn around.

Focus

Without focus, you will never finish. I find the Lindenberg's story to be one of the best illustrations of how focus can lead and keep you on the path of success.

Lindbergh, Charles Augustus (1902-1974), an American aviator, made the first solo nonstop flight across the Atlantic Ocean on May 20-21, 1927. Other pilots had crossed the Atlantic before him, but Lindbergh was the first person to do it alone nonstop.

From New York to Paris (nonstop) in 33 hours, 30 minutes, he made a statement to the press. He said, "At a point, I considered going back, but when I examined the fuel gauge, I realized the remaining fuel could only take me across, not back, so I maintained."

Lindbergh's feat gained him immediate international fame. The press named him "Lucky Lindy" and the "Lone Eagle."

Nothing destroys focus like options.

Nothing frustrates the success of a plan like the mindfulness of plan B.

If there is an imploring alternative to your dream, then trust me, you will soon leave the idea.

Follow your dream as if there were no choices; your life depends on it. Narrow in your focus; deal with distractions.

Keep your eyes on the eight ball. It may be tough, but it's attainable if you don't abandon it for other options.

Stay focused, burn the boats

When they arrived, he ordered his men to burn the ships. I wonder the thoughts in their minds as Cortés promptly thrust his sword. Successful people think differently; they start with the end in mind; unsuccessful people start with the beginning and never see the end.

Here's the lesson: Retreat is easy when you have the option; always see the end first.

Let that marinate in your mind for a minute.

We all cling to something that acts as our escape plan or our exit strategy. It's our safety net; "the just in case factor" is the biggest dream killer…"

Our thought tells us, "This is my safety exit, just in case *things go out of hand*." You immediately lack momentum and register a failure that was waiting to happen.

We delay action until we no longer have fear. Aside from that, our actions are narrow attempts never intended to succeed.

What are your ships? Why are you afraid to let go? Let that ruminate in your mind and write them down? What ship do you need to burn NOW? Trust me, success is in the "now" and not in the tomorrow.

The longer you ponder to act, the more likely you will never do it. What makes it hard to burn your boats is mostly the fear of the unknown called the comfort zone.

John C Maxwell, my mentor, talks about success. For success to happen, your comfort zone must be disturbed.

Nothing makes sense like burning the boats to feel good afterward.

Most of the things we call obstacles are placed there by ourselves, and we ask, "Oh why?" No one packaged it for you; it was your decision not to do the things that create change like burning the boats.

What Cortés did was to cancel the retreat option and create a NEW mindset to succeed or die, which takes us to another resounding trait of success - CHARACTER.

Character is bigger than death; that's the only reason why this story will never die. Cortés doesn't need a tombstone to be remembered.

Roosevelt described character as the decisive factor in the life of an individual that brings honor. Character speaks without words. Your character gives weight to your words; your life becomes your words. Successful leaders never get their reward in the beginning.

"Life chooses what we go through, but we decide how we sail through it." - Maxwell Adekoje

Live every day like today is your last time to impact lives.

You have greatness in you, and you have more than enough to become a person of value. The world badly needs you. Find your purpose and live a life of fulfillment.

BIOGRAPHY

Maxwell's life is a story about hard work, endurance, and inspiration. Originally born in Nigeria, Max first traveled to the United States at a young age, with just $20 in his pocket, seeking the American dream. Like so many who began their working life and career in a new land, the first venture in Max's career in the US was not particularly a great success. Ultimately, there were several failed attempts, but each one along the way served to grow his ambition and sense of belief in the promise of the US and what it could offer to him as a businessman and professional.

First working at a car wash, a restaurant, and numerous other entry-level jobs, Max would regularly sleep three hours daily for years at a time. He was still paying tons of bills, working long hours, and was ultimately unhappy. Despite these challenges, Max never gave up on America and the promise it offered to a young man with a dream and a readiness to realize it with hard work.

Despite this, Max encountered a moment of truth driving home from work one day. So tired in his car, he fell asleep at the wheel, crashed and nearly killed himself. It was at this moment that he knew he needed to change gears in order to change his situation and pursue a life that would deliver him the rewards he deserved.

He wanted to pursue a real American dream, the one that led him to America in the first place and not the one of him washing cars as when he first arrived.

This was when he began exploring ways to grow his own business and grow his net worth. It was around this time he found out about multilevel marketing. Having resolved to chase down a new life for himself, soon after this new career path crystalized, Max was achieving great success in his new field.

Today, he is a top sponsor with numerous awards accredited to his name. He is also the CEO of his own MLM company. Recognized as an international training coach and speaker, Max is proud to be a member of the John C Maxwell Team. While Max is delighted by his success today, he remains hungry for more and goes to work each day with the intention of doing better than ever.

CONTACT INFORMATION

Phone 757-235 6978
Email tmc@mytaprootmc.com

Chapter 10

THE FIRST TIME I FAILED IN MY LIFE WAS THE DAY I WAS BORN

By Kate Jones

I was born a girl, not a boy, and that was a huge disappointment to my father. As I grew up and became more self-aware, it became apparent that every time my father looked at me, there was a cloud of disappointment hanging over him. And as children do, I tried to make myself into the person that I thought he wanted me to be, believing that I would make him proud of me. So, I grew up attempting to be someone else and trying to please others. It was hard, and with each passing year, I buried my true self under layer upon layer of pretending to be someone else until the point where I began to believe the lie and lost sight of the real me.

I felt the only thing I was good at was being a failure, but deep down inside was a part of me that stubbornly refused to give up. There was a small voice deep within me that kept whispering, "I'm here. The real, true you. Let me out so I can be the person I was meant to be."

I refused to listen.

I continued to hide away and tried to be someone I wasn't.

So why am I telling you all this?

The title of this book is Success Unlimited, and here I am talking about abject failure.

Well, there comes a point in everyone's life where we draw a line in the sand, where the pain of being where we are now far outweighs the fear of any change. I reached that point. I had this toxic relationship with money. I desperately wanted more of it, but I hated the fact that no matter what I did, there was never enough. I eventually ended up in deep financial shit, stuck in an abusive relationship and in the depths of despair.

It seemed I was always destined to fail. And therein lay my problem. What I failed to understand was the Law of Attraction - like attracts like. Negativity attracts negativity. A belief in self-failure attracts failure. Limiting self-beliefs attract limiting results. When you constantly focus on the things you DON'T have right now, you will NEVER see the things you CAN have because the universe can only give you what you are focusing on RIGHT NOW.

Now, before you roll your eyes and tell me I'm going all "woo woo" on you, hear me out. Everything I am about to tell you now has its basis in quantum physics. Yep, that's right. Proven, researched, scientific fact. I am no scientist, and I won't go into a load of technical stuff about neutrons, electrons, positrons, etc. We, humans, are all, at our most basic cellular level, nothing more than pure energy. That's a scientifically proven fact. We are vibrating at various frequencies, positivity being high vibration and negativity being low vibration. That's also a scientifically proven fact. We have a measurable energy field around and within us. Guess what... that's a scientifically proven fact as well. Quantum scientists (Einstein included) have proven that all physical matter is made up of energy packets that are not bound by space and time. This energy field has no well-defined boundaries. Science has also proven that the mind has no boundaries.

So where does all this lead in terms of success? I'll take you back to the Law of Attraction. Like attracts like. What if, instead of being negative, and filling our lives with thoughts of failure, desperation and wanting things we don't have, we were to focus on the positive, look at and be grateful for the things we DO have and make the decision to love ourselves instead of allowing feelings of despair and failure?

How do you think that might change things? Surely, if the negativity in the past has brought about only more negativity, doesn't it stand to reason that positivity should bring about more positivity? Surely, if we are happy, we will attract more happiness? If we are grateful for the things we DO have, surely, we will get even more of those things? What if we put out feelings of self-love? Won't we get more love back? The answer to all of those questions is YES. The Universe only knows how to answer YES. Whatever you put out there you will get a YES back.

Negativity will return negativity. Believing you are a failure will only give you more failure. Worrying about debt will only bring more debt. Thinking you will always be alone means you WILL always be alone. Do you get the picture?

THIS WAS THE MASSIVE TURNING POINT IN MY LIFE.

I finally realized that the person solely responsible for everything negative that happened and was happening in my life was me. Boy, that was a really hard lesson to learn. Gone were all my excuses that blamed others. Gone was my justification for being angry with my father, my ex-husband and even my abusive partner.

Shit!!!!

It was ALL DOWN TO ME. Now notice, I'm not saying it was all my FAULT. I am not blaming anyone for where I ended up, not even myself. Blame is a negative vibration that only leads back to more negativity.

Instead, I've accepted that I did not make mistakes for which I could blame myself. I merely made decisions that had a different outcome to the one that I expected. And I made those decisions from a point of not knowing any better.

What this means is that success is available to every one of us. We must change our mindset, change our perspective and change who we are. We need to learn to control our natural monkey-brain that wants us to conform to what we have always experienced, to be who we have always been and to stay in our (dis)comfort zone. At this point, I am going to ask you a question. What is it you truly, deeply want? And what is it that is stopping you from achieving it? Do you want wealth, time, freedom, family time, abundance in your life, peace, contentment, fun, joy, health, to travel the world, to do whatever you want, be whoever you want, be the best possible version of yourself?

I don't think I can hear anyone saying "no" at this point. So, what is it that's stopping you from having all that? Limiting self-beliefs? Fear of failure? Disbelief? Thinking that it's only possible for other better people? Feeling you are not worthy of having all that? I can't afford to do it? I don't want to leave my comfort zone; it's too scary? What if I were to say that all those excuses were just your monkey-brain trying to protect you? What if I was to say you CAN have all of that and it's quite simple. Well, I've got news for you (and this is the MASSIVE lesson I learned that has utterly and completely changed my life).

The Universe (remember that scientifically proven stuff we talked about earlier) only knows how to say YES. So, if you ask for money, health, happiness, love, soul-mate, success, peace, fulfillment, and whatever else you want in life, what do you think you are going to get?

Now I'll put a rider in here; it's not just a case of saying "OK Universe I want blah blah blah" and expecting to get it.

Remember the Law of Attraction?

Like attracts like.

If you want someone to love you, then you must learn to love yourself first.

If you want to receive love, give it first.

If you want more money, be grateful for every penny that is currently in your bank account.

You MUST develop a different mindset.

You must learn to believe in yourself and the fact that you CAN have everything you want.

Practice deliberate thoughts and intentions (positive ones not negative ones).

Clear out all the negative junk from your mind and your life (including negative people). Surround yourself with like-minded, positive, and supportive people.

Develop a positive mindset and wealth consciousness.

Be thankful for everything you have RIGHT NOW and stop focusing on the things you don't have. Become "I am" not "I am not." Become the person you want to be NOW, don't wait.

Educate yourself on how you can achieve the level of mindfulness that brings about true joy, wealth and abundance. Read, read, and read!

Start your day being grateful for everything in your life.

Every. Single. Thing.

Every. Single. Morning.

This is NON-NEGOTIABLE.

If you want the Universe to give you everything, start by being grateful for everything you already have. Apart from being the start of getting all those things you want, it actually makes you feel positive and happy.

When you are grateful and happy, it is IMPOSSIBLE to feel fear. (Again, a scientifically proven fact. Our brain is incapable of feeling fear and gratitude/love at the same time). If you have no fear, you can achieve absolutely anything in life.

Become acutely aware of your subconscious and what it is doing. Your subconscious is responsible for all your self-sabotaging habits, from your beliefs, values, emotions, habits, imagination, and intuition. Learn to become very aware of what your subconscious is thinking and doing because most of your self-limiting beliefs, negative values, feelings, and emotions come from your subconscious and you are not even aware of it.

Learn to listen to what it is doing and correct any negativity.

Stop all negative thoughts in their tracks and replace them with positive ones.

Stop all self-sabotaging thoughts and activities.

Raise your self-awareness to a much higher level, one that you can manage and control. Mindfulness and self-awareness are the two key things to remember and work on.

I am living proof that you CAN change your life dramatically for the better and I want to reach out to as many people as possible and show them and YOU that you don't have to remain in a poverty mindset, facing failure over and over again and feeling utterly shit about yourself.

It is ABSOLUTELY possible to change your life and have everything you ever wanted.

Success is NOT just about money. True happiness, wealth, abundance, and ultimately success comes from WITHIN YOU. It comes from aligning yourself to the one thing that connects everything and everyone – the Universe (remember it's scientifically proven and not woo woo!).

It comes from gratitude, giving and belief that you ARE worthy of having everything you want in life.

It comes from one simple decision to make a change. Don't you owe it to yourself to become the best possible version of yourself? Become the joyous, abundant, wealthy, healthy, grateful person that you have the opportunity to be.

I want you to feel the sheer joy that floods my life every moment. Even when I have moments of doubt or worry, I know how to deal with them, embrace them, analyze them, and then let them go.

I want you to have the wealth consciousness that will deliver you the financial freedom and peace you want, and deserve.

I want you to have the positive mindset that will give you courage, strength, optimism, belief, and gratitude for everything you have right now.

I want you to stop worrying about tomorrow's problems and start enjoying the peace and beauty of today, knowing that your future is secured.

I want you to understand that you CAN have everything you want and that ultimately you can have unlimited success in every single aspect of your life. And above all, I want you to learn to love yourself and know that you are loved in return.

The Universe only knows how to say YES.

What do you want it to say YES to today?

Biography

Kate Jones is a 55-year-old single mother and grandma who finally decided enough was enough. A lifelong self-limiting view of never being good enough in any sphere of life led to a decision to take a totally radical and different approach to life. What followed was a powerful process of personal growth and spirituality that has led to massive life changes and a mission to help others achieve the same.

Contact Information

Facebook https://www.facebook.com/kate.jones.55
YouTube https://www.youtube.com/channel/UCfDJBUR7J_tGR40xzVSRF4g
Instagram https://www.instagram.com/katejonesonline/
Website https://www.katejonesonline.com/

Chapter 11

REDEFINING MY DEFINITION OF SUCCESS

By Arlene Binoya-Strugar, Psy.D.

Success can be defined in a variety of ways. I define it by the ability to evolve and grow mentally and emotionally, an arduous journey I went through beginning in my early childhood. My journey forced me to reevaluate the way I operate in relationships (specifically attachment), internalizing pain, reimagining my self-worth, and ultimately redefining my definition of success.

My original idea of success caused me to chase a goal that wouldn't make me happy. My idea of success can be attributed to how I was raised and the relationship I had with my parents. Separation of parents can have an emotional and behavioral impact on children. Children can become insecure. Aided with love and encouragement from my parents despite their separation, and from other caregivers, over time, led me to develop a healthy self-image and confidence. I have learned and evolved the way I attach to people in relationships, which has allowed me to embrace a path of healing. It's not a perfect method, and by no means, a "one size fits all" process, but what I am about to share with you has afforded me knowledge and courage to know myself better and become the best version of myself.

Attachment

The foundation for our self-image, how we view and value relationships, and how we cope with stressful situations in our life can be attributed to relationships in our early childhood. Attachment is one of these factors and is the primary function in a relationship.

Psychologist Mary Ainsworth says, "Attachment is a deep and enduring emotional bond that connects one person to another across time and space." Attachment and dependableness are a child's basic needs, so they ask these questions: Are you there for me? Am I worthy of your love and attention? Will you be there for me when I need you? The way these questions are answered develops the child's attachment style, views on relationships, emotional maturity, and decision making, which ultimately formulates a person's definition of success.

Ainsworth lists four attachment styles:
1. The secure attachment style. This attachment style has a positive view of self and positive view of others.
2. The insecure avoidant style has a positive view of self and negative view of others.
3. The insecure ambivalent type has a negative view of self and positive view of others.
4. The fourth attachment style, the disorganized attachment style has a negative view of self and negative view of others.

According to Clinton and Sibcy, "People with secure attachment styles believe that they are worthy of love, trust others and expect them to reciprocate love back to them. On the contrary, people with insecure attachment styles push people away and close themselves off emotionally to others in fear of abandonment. They're controlled by the pain in their lives and often question their self-worth."

Emotional scars are injuries, and even though they're not visible, they still take time to heal. When left unattended, like injuries, they become worse, infected, more painful, damage our lives in ways we may not even be aware of.

According to Clinton and Sibcy, "Healthy communication is a great immunizer. A healthy, open communication allows us to heal from attachment and emotional injuries by talking openly and honestly about our feelings. Internalizing and reflecting on our pain helps us distance the event from emotion and process facts. It allows us to use finite words to describe our failures, allowing us to move on and reframe the meaning of our lingering pain into a process of healing. We can reframe our feelings, or simply just let out and verbally release them. We can process a healthier way of coping with our pain, which leads us to the last process of healing - forgiveness."

Clinton and Sibcy further state "Whether it is forgiving ourselves or someone else, acceptance is the closing of the wound. Like on the body, even though remnants of the injury are still there and leave a mark, we are able to move on with our lives. Healing from attachment and emotional wounds is not about forgetting, it's about accepting, learning and moving on. It allows us to trust again and frees us from pain."

Cultural Identity and Self-Identity

Our culture shapes social norms, values, morals, and traditions which are inseparable from us. People are shaped by their culture and culture is shaped by them. I view my success on how my society preforms collectively. Harmony and interdependence are characteristics I value more. My success is determined by the success of the group to which I belong. It is a group effort, and each member is given the same value and recognition. A very eastern view, yes, but I was able to merge it with a very individualistic idea of success as well.

On the contrary, self-reliance and independence are greatly valued in an individualistic culture. Western cultures prioritize the success of the individual, despite the effort of the group. Both have their pros and cons, but while still heavily having a collective view of success, I am able to incorporate individualistic aspects of success which help me overcome aspects of my leadership style and mindset that could be interpreted as limiting.

Behavioral Change: Brain, Mind, Body

Daniel Amen, a renowned neuropsychiatrist, says "When your brain works right, you work right. When your brain is in trouble, you have troubles in life." Amen has conducted thousands of single-photon emission computed tomography (SPECT) brain scans and has discovered formulas that are harmful and helpful to our brains.

The Amen Clinic has listed many things that can hurt our brain:

- Brain injuries
- Drugs and alcohol
- Obesity
- Sleep apnea
- Smoking/caffeine
- Diabetes
- Hypertension
- Toxins
- Low Vitamin D, thyroid, testosterone, blood sugar

- Poor diets/sugar
- Stress/depression
- Lack of exercise
- Poor decisions
- Unhealthy peer groups
- Not knowing your own brain.

Brain habits that can help heal our brain are:
- Good decisions
- Conscientiousness
- Positive peer groups
- Protecting the brain
- Clean environment
- Physical health/exercise/healthy diet
- Healthy weight
- Eight hours of sleep a night
- New learning
- Killing automatic negative thoughts
- Omega 3s
- Gratitude
- Stress management.

Although I've listed the good and bad things for your brain, it's not that simple. Changing habits and behaviors is hard work, and it's even harder to break habits we aren't even aware of. Many of us associate failures with the lack of willpower, not enough motivation, weakness of character, or personality flaws to make changes in our lives; however, it's not because we don't know the negative effects of our bad habits, but because we don't know how to change.

James and Janice Prochaska constructed six stages to guide us to change our bad habits.
1. Precontemplation - I am not ready; not intending to take action in the next six months
2. Contemplation - I am getting ready; intending to take action in the next six months
3. Preparation - I am ready; ready to take action in the next 30 days

4. Action - I have made the behavior change but for less than six months
5. Maintenance - I am doing the new healthy behavior for more than six months
6. Termination - I am confident with the change, not tempted to relapse

By implanting all of these schools of thoughts, I have been able to change my outlook on life and relationships, heal from old emotional wounds, and reframe my mindset to succeed. I now understand my ways of thinking in groups and as an individual. My leadership style is connected to how I see myself in relation to other members of the group and how I value them. Overall, I am able to see the synergistic relationships between our habits, and how it affects our health (brain, mind, and body) and the quality of our lives.

Biography

From her humble beginnings, Arlene Binoya-Strugar, Psy.D. never quit. As a social scientist, she not only has a deeper understanding of human behavior but also has applied these teachings into her life. She used her personal experiences, educational and cultural background to increase her emotional and social intelligence in leading groups and to understand human aspirations. She is a social scientist with a passion for understanding human pain and experiences to improve human lives and existence.

Contact Information

Facebook: https://www.facebook.com/braingysticsintegrative
LinkedIn: https://www.linkedin.com/in/arlene-strugar-psy-d-a635602/
Website: www.braingystics.com

Chapter 12

5 STEPS TO BECOMING A GOOD ENTREPRENEUR

By Jasmina Cernilogar Mihajlovic

Have you ever asked someone what he or she thinks about you? How does he see you?

Do you want to know why people treat you like they do?

What if you asked people what they think about your work?

Maybe you are scared to hear the truth, and it seems easier to hide and be invisible.

If you have asked, then you know how it feels and if you haven't you should try.

It's worth the try. I am always surprised and honored because people around me see me like the person I always wanted to be. They see my dreams and my fears. It's nice to hear from people that I live my dreams.

People often tell me, it's so easy for you, you are so confident, you know what you are doing, or you are so determined and always find a way.

Who, me? Are they really talking about me? It's like I don't know that person. I am a little girl who doesn't know how to react and then when no one does anything I try to find a way. I am not confident. I am just determined to succeed; I want to make a better day, a better year and a better world for everybody.

I can share my knowledge and help people. I can share my experience and my common sense to help people from stress so that they don't go through the tough times I did. Maybe, I can help them think differently and open their mind to positive and beautiful things in life and business. It's bigger and stronger than me.

Many times, I want to quit, and I hide from everybody, but it's always just for a short time. I am here to tell what I must tell. I want to change the world.

My mission is to teach common people how to be an entrepreneur and how to organize their administrative activities, books, taxes, money, and finances. I enjoy every moment of it.

From idea to business success is a long journey. Nobody can do it for you. You'll have to do it yourself.

Everything starts with your first few steps. I've done things differently for more than 15 years. I've had to figure out a lot of things through trial and error.

You must learn new things constantly, be focused, determined, and not fear failure. If you fail, try again till you succeed.

If you have an idea, project, or a dream; and want to become an entrepreneur, you have to go through these five steps and learn the fundamentals of entrepreneurship.

1. How to open a company
2. How to do business
3. Costs
4. Business report
5. Marketing

Let's discuss the five steps in more detail.

Step #1: How to open a company

The laws are different depending on your country. You may need to get familiar with the rules in your country, the costs, the benefits, and your applicable taxes.

It's important to understand the taxes you need to pay, your obligations on book-keeping, invoicing, employment, etc.

Understand as much as you can before you start your business. It's important to do your due diligence, understand the laws in your country, and ask as many questions as possible before you even start.

Step #2: How to do business

This step involves taking care of administrative activities, organizing work processes, making sure that you have enough finances, opening a bank account, calculating profit margins, doing your bookkeeping, handling taxes, dealing with clients, suppliers, and employees.

It might be hard to think about all the activities in your business before you even start. You might want to figure things out along the way, but the process will be less painful if you prepare yourself. Preparation will help you stay more focused on your business without losing time and energy figuring out processes while you are on the run.

Step #3: Costs

An entrepreneur needs to know his costs. He should find legal ways to reduce taxes. He should know the difference between costs, expenses, outflows, revenues, and inflows.

Distinguishing between these terms is important. Not knowing these terms can land you in trouble. It's like driving a car blindfolded.

Imagine your business is doing great, you have several orders, you are selling good, but if you are not going to track your expenses and revenues, you will never know about the financial health of your business. So, learn about economics, read stories about other entrepreneurs, imitate them until you are ready to innovate and experiment with new things on your own.

Step #4: Understand business reports

As an entrepreneur, you will need to deal with banks, clients, and suppliers. It's important to understand the language of business and know the rules of the game.

It's important to know the difference between a balance sheet, income statement, cash flow statement, capital gains report, and how you could optimize these for your business.

You may not be an expert in economics, and you need not become one. But you must know at least the basics of running your business.

It's your business, and the responsibility of its success depends entirely on you. A startup is like a newborn baby, and you'll have to nurture it through the delicate initial stages where the business can be vulnerable. You can't learn everything, but you can gain just enough knowledge necessary to understand the fundamentals of business and economics.

You may think that you can do without it. But I suggest that you learn as much as you can before you start. A few mistakes can set you back by several years. I believe knowledge is everything and a person without knowledge is at a significant disadvantage.

Step #5: Marketing

You might have a great product, but what if no one knows about it? Marketing is one of the most important cornerstones of a successful business. All you do, write and say about you and your company is marketing.

You have to find the most appropriate way to inform people about your business. Your customers must like you and your product. My coach Lenja says "You must first tattoo yourself in your client's hearts and then their wallets."

You need to know some things about internet sites and how you can spread the word about your business. You have to learn a lot about social networks and how to use it for your business.

Advertising is the key to success today. How can you use it for your business to attract more clients?

You have to think about your marketing plan, and maybe you don't even know what it is.

It's not enough to just have a business idea, but you should also have a strategy on how to do it. And to do it you need the knowledge that makes you better and more prepared than your competitors.

These are just a few things you should know about entrepreneurship before you start. I have to admit I didn't even know half of it when I began. If I did, my entrepreneurial life would've been much easier, and I would've reached my goals much faster.

My sincere suggestion to all of you is to chase your dreams, don't stop if you come across obstacles because there will always be something that seems difficult to overcome. Everything can be done. Things that seem impossible are not always impossible. Things will come to you if you truly desire them, work on it, and don't let other people discourage you.

Fortune favors the brave. That's the entrepreneur in me talking.

BIOGRAPHY

Jasmina Cernilogar Mihajlovic is an entrepreneur with a heart. She's been running a tax consulting and accounting business for the last 15 years. Her mission is to teach people to become good entrepreneurs. She has her own way of giving knowledge that comes from her experience of helping several entrepreneurs.

Contact Information

LinkedIn: https://www.linkedin.com/in/jasmina-%C4%8Dernilogar-m-a5941552/
Twitter: https://twitter.com/jasminacermih
Instagram: https://www.instagram.com/jasminacernilogarmihajlovic/

CHAPTER 13

LIVING AN INSPIRED, PURPOSEFUL, AND AMAZING LIFE

By Jeremy Hoort

My family was as far from normal as it gets, with my two Fathers both working as drug dealers until I was 13 years old, but still, I grew up surrounded by love, faith, and discipline.

After I turned 13, my biological Father went to Federal Prison, while my other Father chose to follow a different path, one that I consider being much harder. He gave it all up, the drugs and the crime, and instead focused his efforts on his faith. For a while, we lived relatively happily, albeit modestly, until the divorce of my father and mother.

After the divorce, my mother took care of three children all by herself. Neither of my Fathers supported us financially. And so, from a young age, I started to learn about the corruption of people, governments, police, and I began to see what money does to people and society. It's destructive.

My life was like something most people only see in the movies – we would hide silver and gold bars in our laundry baskets and wait until we could launder it through a business. We were constantly playing cat and mouse with the police and the federal government.

In a way though, I was lucky, because despite the illegal activity, my siblings and I were always loved. We were always disciplined and taught right from wrong. And I was also lucky that my fathers weren't tied to any organized crime, so they were able to walk away.

My biological Father served five years in a federal prison for possession of 200 pounds of marijuana. He was set up by his own friends in a federal sting operation. While he could have shortened his sentence, he served full time, because he refused to snitch on others, and for this, I was proud of him. He did the crime, without tattling on others to get a lighter sentence.

My Step-Father raised me while my biological Father was in prison, and I consider him just as much a Father as my real Dad. He made the hard decision to give up the illegal life for good and left the drug trade after finding his faith in the bible.

I plan on writing a detailed book about my Fathers and my childhood, where I'll divulge all the dirty details, but here I wanted you to see that our lives are about choices and our thoughts. I chose to be the direct opposite of my Fathers when it came to my schooling, career life and my time in the military. I never allowed myself a failure or even sub-par performance, ever. I could have followed in my Father's footsteps and lived a life of crime, chasing cash, but instead, I decided to focus on High School and afterward, on my military career.

I learned that regardless of our history, we choose who we will become. Living in the past, and holding grudges will lead to becoming consumed by negative thoughts. Everyone has one main choice: to be a victim of their circumstances or to take control and be a lion of their own lives. I chose to be a lion and so far, I've reached my goals, and been successful in most aspects of my life.

My life after childhood and high school was one of many tough choices, but by age 18, I was out on my own, and I chose to join the United States Air Force. I only signed a four-year contract, but I made the mistake of not having a lawyer look over that contract, which made be obligated to serve for eight years, if the government needed me. It was a lesson learned that you must be careful what you sign.

I completed four successful years working on the fighter aircraft of an E&E specialist but went to complete a total of 10 years' service, working with and around fighter jets like the F-111 Aardvark fighter-bomber (whispering death), F-16 Fighting Falcon, and F-15 eagle. I also completed five years of extra duty in the Air Force Base Honor Guard.

With commanding officers talking highly of me, and several awards and medals under my belt, I could have returned to the military as a commissioned officer, and that was my initial plan. However, my first son was born just after 9/11, and then my plans changed. Instead of returning to the military, I finished my business degree at the University of South Florida in 2015.

I can honestly say that I think all of my current success is due to me being the best father and husband I could be for my family. I now have three beautiful boys: Bryce, Grayson, and Vander who are all the light of my life. I also have my wife, Meagan, who is the rock of the family and is the most beautiful and intelligent woman I have ever met. I'm so happy to have her in my life – it looks like my prayers were answered, because I now have my lioness, and I love her more every day.

I think it's important to create our world in our own minds first, and then it's up to us to decide what's important to us as individuals, and what we're going to do in this life. I think we create our futures long before they happen through what we think and how we act, so keep those negative and limiting thoughts away from your creativity.

Now that I have achieved my success, and created my perfect family, I now try to make a difference on a local level. I started Dash Health Consulting so that I could make a difference by helping one family or business at a time.

We all only have one life to live, a life that's ended with a (-) dash. None of us know when that dash is going to come, which is why it's so important to live every important moment.

I was inspired by many family members, mentors, and my faith to create a lasting legacy and make the world a better place so that by the time my dash comes, I've done my bit to help others achieve success and happiness. I want to help the whole person, from health to wealth while allowing individuals to leave a legacy that will last for many future generations. Legacy in this sense isn't just about wealth, in fact, wealth has little to do with it. My legacy will be the life I lead, Legacy may seem like wealth, but that isn't the case at all. My personal legacy will be the life I lead, my family, and the book I leave for my family and sons along with my charity, CHILD Charity USA (www.childcharityusa.com).

CHILD Charity USA stands for:

Children

Health

Investment

Learning

Development

The goal is to educate children about finance and health. We work with schools for a better tomorrow and help deliver education that will help our children to be successful. Denzel Washington once said: "Don't aspire to make a living, aspire to make a difference" and that's what CHILD Charity USA is all about.

Wealth isn't guaranteed, not for me, not for anyone, but I believe that I've already achieved success and that this is just the tip of the iceberg.

I've always been good at numbers, and so I tried to base my corporate career around them, but I struggled to find a career I agreed with. Every role I tried seemed to be based around selling clients services or products that weren't always right for them.

I became fed up with businesses only promoting the products they were able to sell, rather than genuinely helping clients with a dilemma or pointing them in the right direction. So I created Dash Health Consulting so that I could help people succeed, from Health to Wealth. It's a unique business, the first of its kind.

We focus on what the client needs, bringing businesses together to work for and with clients, rather than just promoting one type of product or service. I hope that Dash Health Consulting will disrupt the market and help millions of people succeed. I created a company that has a huge amount of products and services at its fingertips, for those that want to build their own business.

As well as putting entrepreneurs and businesses in touch with the right services, we're also delivering business and finance education through our website. This is something I haven't seen any other financial advisor, company or business do! I am so excited to share my one-of-a-kind company with the nation.

I'm writing my book to inspire others to focus not on instant rewards, but on the journey towards success. Everywhere you look, you'll see people trying to sell 'get rich quick' schemes that don't necessarily work, but I expect more. I believe that by helping each other as well as ourselves, we'll solve a lot of nationwide issues, and we can all benefit and find our success together. If all you want is a way to make quick money, so you can live the life of a millionaire, I suggest buying a lotto ticket and a prayer.

We need to make new services and products that don't just help one person or business. There's some amazing technology out there that can be used to make this world a better place; it's only our own creativity that's limiting us.

Is success based on a paper currency and the ability to hoard as much as we can as quickly as we can, not caring what it might do to others? Sure, pursuing money might work short term but what kind of damage will we be cleaning up? I believe we'll find ourselves back where we were in 2008, with more bubbles in the economy.

My book and my business aren't about get-rich-quick plans; they're about the truth and a different way of looking at things. I've built a business that offers a number of solutions to a huge number of people.

The business world today is a house of cards, and if you don't just want to take my word for it, there are many other experts much smarter than myself warning us that it's unstable. The trouble is that no one wants to admit it, because admitting it would make the economy even more delicate. But it is bad, and we need to admit this to ourselves so that we can move on to a more controlled economy.

I was once good at poker. I could have pursued it further, but I chose to help others first. I might play poker again one day, but I fully understand that it's gambling. What I don't understand is how people can think the stock market is any different. Rather than putting money into gambling, I believe people should be looking to create products that protect the economy and earn money as well. There are so many different ways to do this, so many different ways to protect people first, and genuinely help them, rather than just selling regardless.

We all have greatness inside us, and we can all excel in life, we just have to access our talents, develop them, and put them to use. Your job doesn't define who you are, it's just a means to an end, a tool.

I challenge you to live an inspired, purposeful, and amazing life. Your life is a ship that only you can captain. Remember not to view failures as a bad thing, think of them as clues. Each failure is a clue that you're heading in the wrong direction, and in its own way, it will steer you in the right direction.

Listen to the strangest secret by Earl Nightingale.

"Do not go where the path may lead, go instead where there is no path and leave a trail." - Ralph Waldo Emerson

Biography

With over 20 years of experience in customer service, ten years of USAF Honor Guard structure, Jeremy Hoort brings amazing talent, taking care of the client from health to wealth to a whole new level. The one of a kind platform of experts in one location at https://www.dashhealthconsulting.com/–is truly unique and inspiring. It changes lives forever while giving back through their charity CHILDcharityUSA.com.

Contact Information

Facebook https://www.facebook.com/jeremy.hoort
LinkedIn https://www.linkedin.com/in/live4life/
Twitter https://twitter.com/ReachDashDCH
YouTube https://www.youtube.com/channel/UCM9A0b9JTL41t TEWYD7OGVQ
Instagram https://www.instagram.com/reachdashdhc/
Website https://www.dashhealthconsulting.com/
Blog https://jeremyhoort.wixsite.com/website
Pinterest https://www.pinterest.com/craighoort/
Charity https://www.childcharityusa.com

Chapter 14

I AM NOTHING. YET, I HAVE EVERYTHING

By Maiko Johanson

I am so deeply honored to share my humble thoughts in this chapter. In this eye-opening journey, let these wonderful people be your guides on the way to your unlimited success.

As we enter this life, naked and unaware of what lies beyond, we have already decided to be successful because we won the first race to be born.

As we grow, we are full of wonder and excitement about learning something new every day.

Our self-image is, "I am enough," "I am successful in everything I do," "I am awesome," "life is wonderful."

What we don't know is the fact that we observe the environment we are in, and it will form our way of thinking and acting. This first part of our personality, until the age of six or so, will remain with us. The most significant part of our belief system is developed by the example of our parents, siblings, attitudes, thought patterns and the immediate environment in which we live.

Then, as we develop an acceptable way of independent thinking, we are sent to an educational system where everything changes. It is the beginning of a careful molding of our minds and a new belief system about how life should go and should be lived. We dream, and we want to be somebody else; we choose role models, and we start acting like them, thinking it's cool and that is our identity, that might be a part of our essence, and we get lucky to become who we were meant to be. But, that's not the way it actually works out for the majority of people.

We start to lose the mindset that "I am more than enough." We grow, learn, get a job, etc.

We seek; we dream; we experience the magic and the ugliness of life.

First, all is well. We work hard for a better future; we hear stories about success, fancy things, different possibilities and lifestyles we want for our lives as well, but nothing changes. We don't feel content; we start to question things; we try to make ourselves feel better by consuming alcohol, drugs and junk food to give us little relief or to numb us down. Years go by, and we are stuck in the system that sold us an idea that there is freedom in entrepreneurship and that is possible for us, but most of us are blind to see that we are now modern-day slaves.

We have developed negative self-talk in our heads about us, and we are troubled in our heads how others see us. Questions like "Am I enough to do this" and "Am I capable for this and that," will take over, and we find ourselves lost in our own lives. We still have dreams about a better future, but we don't realize the negative ball of energy that is now growing bigger.

We start to be a victim and blame others; we start to talk about people behind their backs. Life sucks, and we need to escape.

We don't realize the power of thought and feeling because nobody teaches us that in school.

We don't know the laws of the universe and the power behind them. We are at a breaking point in our lives where usually something happens. This point in our lives can make us or break us. If we are shaken up properly, we might gain some new energy for the understanding that we need to change our lives, our selves, and that we have the power to do so.

I broke my back six times before I needed to go to surgery. It changed my view of life. I had to go to Peru into the Amazon jungle and take part in a one-week Ayahuasca retreat to lose the pain I had been carrying with me since my childhood. I learned a lot, and it made another change in my personality. I felt free, but I still lacked the confidence to step up another level in my actions. I got malaria and almost died before I woke up, to realize that I needed to love more deeply the family and closest friends I have.

I now understand deeply that I have only one life, and I need to be true to my calling. We don't have to go through so many painful and scary experiences to realize we are the architect of our life. Maybe we accidentally stumble on some motivational video or a book that changes our view of life, and we take action to change our lives because the old ways are simply not getting us anywhere. From this realization of an awakened mind, we pray for a better future and, because we had a rough path, we feel hope, and that changes us to feel better and attract better thoughts.

Like attracts like is a combination of words we grow up with, but we do not give it any real attention until we are pushed towards it. Here I, talk to the people who understand my thoughts or who want to understand. I talk to you, someone who is looking for a change, and that very reason is why you are reading this book. You want and need changes in your life, and you are developing your thinking to the point where you know that you don't know about things, but you need to know more for the change to come. This place in one's thoughts is magical, because you have changed your vibration just by realizing something, and that something gives you power.

A person creates their life just by thought. Whether or not you believe it does not matter because it is the truth, and if you just take the time to think deeply about it, you will realize that. Like attracts like, so your thoughts will attract like-minded thoughts, and that process will grow.

You should take time to think about your childhood and the dreams you had in the past, to realize that a big part of them have come to manifest already in your life. You just have been blind to see it; you have been like a zombie just staggering through life. We as human beings are all sensitive to the energies around us. We all say things like, "I feel this way," or "I sense that something is going to happen." Think more deeply about what you feel or sense. This is something we cannot see in the physical world, but we can feel it and sense it.

These thoughts will open up a new world, and that world is full of wonder and magic just like when you were a child. It is hard to comprehend at first, but I promise you that your life will change as you let yourself go into the world of thought.

We all have the power to feel, sense and think. If we think about what it means, it all comes back down to energy, vibration or high frequency. They are the same thing. Choose a word that resonates with you and go from there. Feeling and sensing is something we all know but we cannot see, so we call it energy. Thoughts are in our heads. We can hear them but cannot see, so they are energy?

Earl Nightingale said, "We become what we think about most of the time." Think about that; reflect on that; let it sink in. The people that sing think about it most of their time. People who do sports think about it most of the time. The person who thinks about writing becomes a writer. The person who wants to be an artist becomes one. The person who is crazy enough to think that he wants to change the world thinks about that most of the time and eventually is the person who does it. Nobody comes to make them who they want to be or what they want in their life; there is no savior. You are your own savior; you are the change; you have the power to change things in your life, and it all starts by thinking.

It is something so simple, and that is why it's hard to grasp at first, but as you start to play with that idea, you will notice the changes in your thoughts. You don't have to know how to do the change - you just have to think about it and feel good about it; this is all you need to do. As you think, you will attract more like-minded thoughts. Like-minded thoughts will attract like-minded people. We all have experienced and heard, "I felt so drawn towards that person," and "We had such good chemistry."

Like attracts like; it is energy! Like-minded people together form a mastermind as it is taught by Napoleon Hill, and from that, things start to change. I truly believe that, because I have known it in me, I have sensed it in me. I did not have the intellectual skills to explain it, but I knew this was something to learn about. I started reading all the self-development books I could get my hands on, and I started to look into the science by going through books to explain all of that to me in a little bit more detail.

The science behind everything does not matter; what matters is what you want. Think about your thoughts; start to be the observer of your mind; start to write things down to get clarity about your thoughts. You become self-aware; that will grant you a gift of patience and understanding of how unaware you have been before. You start to see the negative thought patterns, and you start to know you can reprogram your thoughts into positive ones.

This book is filled with golden nuggets of wisdom that will help you to make the change in your life if you truly want it! The fact that you are reading this book is a powerful step toward your future, and I salute you for that. It does not matter how far you have gone in your personal life or how successful you are in your business. We all have self-doubt at some level; we all are afraid of something. I am here to tell you that you will be alright; everything will be alright; you just have to believe in yourself! I believe in you! You are enough! You are a beautiful human being! We all have things we are not happy with about ourselves, but that is what makes us humans, that makes us unique, that makes us perfect as we are!

The best advice I can give you is to "develop self-awareness." You can do this by turning off the tv and just go for a walk, or simply sit in silence and marinate in your thoughts within yourself and listen. Be mindful about what is going on. Just observe and learn. It is quite hard to do at first, but you will get better at it! Develop your intellect by reading books; it will open up understanding about your own psychology. Eat good organic food; take care of your body. Meditate, and the biggest gifts you can offer yourself are compassion, patience, forgiveness, and self-love. It will make your inner self feel better and, from that, your whole perspective of life will reflect back to you in your reality.

If you want to change things in your life, change things in your life! You have that power!

If I could do it, then I am more than certain that you can do it, too.

I wish and pray for self-awareness, self-love, compassion, forgiveness, and patience to all the people in the world.

Biography

Maiko Johanson believes that everything in life will fall into place without labels.

He is a seeker, writer, son, brother, uncle, a friend, a man, and a world traveler. He believes that he is nothing, yet he has everything.

Contact Information

Facebook: https://www.facebook.com/Maiko.Johanson
YouTube: https://www.youtube.com/channel/UCTO5_OJ_64m2X6_ZYfiHiIA?view_as=subscriber

Chapter 15

HOW TO WORK LESS, EARN MORE AND LIVE FREE AS A LIFESTYLE ENTREPRENEUR

By Francis Ablola

If you spotted me at Starbucks grabbing my morning double espresso or white mocha, you wouldn't think much.

My normal work attire consists of a t-shirt, basketball shorts and a pair of old flip-flops. Chances are I haven't shaved in a week, and my backwards cap is hiding the fact that I desperately need a haircut.

You'd probably never guess I just wrapped up a marketing campaign for one of my clients that brought in an additional 7-figures in revenue, or that I'm masterminding a project that will bring in thousands of new potential customers in just a few weeks.

I operate under the radar, and that's the way I like it.

I call it being a "Lifestyle Entrepreneur."

I work only when I feel like it, with the people I like investing my time with and do it by my own rules from my Floridian beachfront office overlooking the Atlantic Ocean.

The rest of the time you'll find me at home with my beautiful wife and my bouncing baby girl, traveling the country meeting with fellow "Lifestyle Entrepreneurs," and learning new skills that create massive results for my clients and me.

I love what I do, and it's exactly how I designed it.

I don't say this to brag or boost.

I wasn't born with any special talents or advantages.

I tell you this because it's possible for anyone to design a business that supports YOU and your desired lifestyle.

And if you truly want to earn more, work less and enjoy life, then read this special message below.

I'd like to share with you how I went from a 20-something college dropout to corporate burn out, to living a life of AWESOMENESS by design… and how you can do it, too.

Why I Never Want To Grow Up!

It's easy to get lost in what the universe throws at you. Long hours, stressful days, increasing frustration, lost time with family and friends – when you're not in "control of your world," you accept this as status quo.

So many people get caught up in the day-to-day, working for a living and forgetting to create a life.

I know this from personal experience.

Starting out in my professional life, I thought I was doing everything the right way.

I had a good job, at a big Fortune 1000 company, with an impressive title, and an office with a window. Check.

I'm all set, and life couldn't be better, or so I thought.

And all of that's fine if that's what you want. But, if you've got the entrepreneurial bug in your DNA, you'll get antsy quickly.

(My guess is if you're reading this right now, then you know what I mean.)

To me, all the hype about the "grown-up life" was a lie.

You do a good job, work longer and longer hours, sit in more and more meetings, and end up spending more than you make.

I got a plaque and certificate of appreciation.

I wanted more than a plaque, a warm place to sit for eight to nine hours a day, 401K and the cost of living raise every year.

I consider myself fortunate that I found out early in my career that I wanted more, and was willing to go get it.

Early Warning Signs

Ever since I was a kid, I've had the "be my own boss" itch. Remember the kid in your neighborhood carrying around a bucket wanting to wash your car, or going door-to-door offering to cut your grass for a few bucks over the summer and on the weekends? Yup, that was me.

And it didn't stop there. At 12 years of age, I had a crew of neighborhood kids going door to door selling our services. We were a growing enterprise. During the week, I hustled selling pixie sticks and bubble gum in the lunch room, a venture not looked upon too kindly by the teachers.

There's a saying that the grade C and D students own businesses, and the A and B students end up working for them.

I'm living proof that this statement is valid. I'm not ashamed to say that I barely made it out of high school and left the university before they could kick me out.

Meanwhile, I was working, learning about business on my own, trying new things, taking risks, taking action and getting results.

Over the years, I've had other ventures... You name it, selling advertising to local shops, web design services, multi-level marketing companies selling everything from gas rebates to groceries online. Some were good; some were bad, some were profitable, some not, but All Learning Experiences.

One of the keys to being an entrepreneur is to be willing to fail forward and do it fast.

I'll admit my first major business attempt after leaving college was a major flop.

I'm thankful for it because I discovered a lot about myself and the people around me, which were both positive.

I was in my early 20's and thought I was unstoppable. I knew it all, and I could do it all.

I had a steady job working for a web development company that I helped build from the ground up, but I got bored and wanted more. (You'll see this is a pattern for entrepreneurs.)

So, I quit with nothing lined up.

To add to the urgency, I had planned in two weeks' time to propose to my high school sweetheart and girlfriend of six years. (She said yes, by the way!)

The next year was filled with uncertainty and total confusion on what I should do next. I filled my days getting my hands on every course, book, and CD and attending every seminar I could to learn how to make my business work.

I took on odd projects; we lived off my new fiancé's first-year teacher salary and racked up thousands on credit cards using advances to pay the rent. I even traded my services for gift certificates to a restaurant.

Yes, I worked for food, literally.

I often tell people the worst thing that can happen if you go out on your own and it doesn't work is you have to get a job.

Well, that's what I did. And because I spent a year developing skills and growing my ability to add value to the marketplace, I made myself more valuable in the workforce which landed me in a prime position using the new skill sets to open career options that a college dropout like me would otherwise not have available.

But by now, you know how I feel about working for someone else. So, as soon as I could, I ventured out on my own again and this time with A New-Found Confidence And Solid Game Plan.

Through my experience, I created a game plan of exactly what I would want my business to look like, and what it would take in time and resources.

My new goal was to create a business that supports my life, and not the other way around. I can, fortunately, say I've thrown out the conventions of traditional business and am operating quietly under the radar and still able to create a fantastic lifestyle for my family.

Here are a few key lessons I've discovered that have allowed me to fulfill my personal and business goals:

Attitude: There's a thin line between success and failure. Winners push beyond past failures; they learn from every experience and use the past to fuel the fire to succeed.

Communication: Your ability to communicate and influence applies in every area of business – working with vendors, team members, clients and, of course, making sales.

Creating a network: Your network equals your net worth. It's often said that your income is a direct result of the five people with whom you spend the most time. I'm a natural introvert, but I've ignored my natural tendencies to build a strong network of top-level players.

Support system: Stop listening to negative people in your life. They won't serve you or help you reach your goals. I've been blessed with a wonderful partner; my wife has been supportive every step of the way. Also, the people I've attracted in my network all share similar goals, and that only serves to push us forward.

Find a mentor: I've been fortunate to have worked with many people who I consider mentors. This is the ultimate shortcut to success – finding someone who has what you want, who's done what you're doing, and who has a proven path to reach your goals.

A business vehicle: What many don't realize is there is so much opportunity just waiting for the armed and ready entrepreneur. You can take your skills and fill a need, or plug into a ready-built system. If the system works, do it.

Risk: Willingness to take calculated risks. Fear stops many people from achieving their goals, but the best way to overcome fear is to face it.

Leverage: Here's the key to freeing yourself from work. Outsource, leverage time and other people's resources. If you don't like doing a repetitive task, don't do it. If you can easily train someone else to take work off your hands, then do it. You'll have more time to work ON your business.

Know your reason why: It's the driver behind everything you do, especially if your goal is to create a lifestyle-driven business.

My *why* is to spend time with my family and enjoy our time together without having to worry about financial restraints. I've been fortunate to be a part of almost every second of my brand-new baby girl's life and watch her grow every day.

This is the lifestyle I've created, by design. And, now that you know it's possible, I hope you will take time to figure out what matters most to you and live your dreams.

Biography

Francis Ablola is a marketing strategist and award-winning business writer. His unique ability to effectively communicate with and influence wide audiences has generated millions in revenue and created tens of thousands of new opportunities for his clients. From Fortune 1000 to garage start-ups, he has been helping companies succeed using highly effective yet unusual advertising.

Chapter 16

YOUR PARTNER IN CRIME: THE SUBCONSCIOUS MIND

By Oliver T. Asaah

What is the subconscious mind?

The subconscious is the guardian angel of the conscious mind and the queen motivator of our actions.

The subconscious influences every second of our lives in everything we do or fail to do; it is dictated by programs that have been systematically installed in our subconscious starting from birth. It is our partner in crime that micromanages the roles we play: actors, participants, or spectators in the theatre of life, as the case may be.

Some of these thoughts are empowering while others are disempowering. Disempowering ideas are those that hold us back from exploring, exploiting, and manifesting our passion and unleashing our full potential. Empowering ones help us get closer to our destiny. Many minds focus on disempowering thoughts.

How is the subconscious programmed?

The subconscious is the invisible master pilot of our actions. It *tele*-guides our thinking; our thinking dictates our actions, and our actions show who we are.

What can we do to shape our subconscious to work for us?

In the Nweh and some other cultures in the Cameroons, twins are believed to possess some magical powers: they can bring good and bad luck to their family. Twins can inadvertently hurt family members by inflicting severe pain mysteriously. Upon satisfying their demand, they mysteriously fix their fetish deeds.

Once upon a time, at the age of six, one of my step twin-sisters was upset with me, and she promised to sprain my leg. She kept staring at my right leg. Consequently, after a while when I stood up, I realized I couldn't walk. My right leg was hurting, so I submitted to her magical powers, coaxing her to forgive me and return my leg to normal. Instantaneously, my leg came back to normal.

This belief, like many others, have existed from time immemorial; it is held to be true and inextricably interwoven with the lifestyle of believers. Some beliefs might not be true, but extreme belief and faith make them seem real to us. The subconscious is programmed similarly.

The subconscious is programmed in three ways: persons (family, teachers, mentors, peers, friends, associates), place (environment) and things (experiences, media, books, films). These three dimensions encode the subconscious at varying degrees. They determine who, how, where, when, why we acquire our programs. These questions will facilitate the process of reprogramming our subconscious.

The programming of our subconscious starts from conception. According to Joseph Susedik, "Talking to children in the womb has a tremendous impact on their development." He recommends a calm, serene environment for a pregnant mother. A solemn atmosphere ensures the birth of a child with utter trust in the parent. The Dallas *Times Herald article, May 15, 1982,* wrote that Joseph and Jitsuko Susedik believed any parent can raise brilliant children; they just need phonics, environment, and curiosity; the earlier, the better. (Ziglar 1985).

"Only if the child has complete trust, can he or she be taught. You must teach your children with love, gentleness, and only at a time they are willing to learn," Susedik says.

Also cited by Ziglar 1985, Dr. Carole Taylor, Ph.D., head of the Tolatr Academy in Pittsburgh, Pa., believes once children master phonics, they can read anything, even college texts. Dr. Taylor has daughters, ages 10 and 14, enrolled part-time in pre-med courses in a community college. She applies the person, place and things factors responsible for programming in empowering her daughters.

How can we access programs in the subconscious?

This is a journey into the realm of our being to enjoy human endowments: self-awareness, imagination, conscience and independent will; that differentiates us from animals. Just 'deep' it: (Dig, Employ, Expect, Profit) and the salt and the sweat will yield the malt.

Unlike consulting a doctor when we are sick for diagnostics and prescriptions, we have to DOCTOR ourselves in reprogramming the subconscious; that has been my experience. To me, DOCTOR means: Diagnose, Operate, Cure, Treat, Oxygenate and Respect. The exercise is very personal, serene and engaging.

"Faith is a state of mind which can be induced through repeated affirmations or instructions to the SUBCONSCIOUS MIND through the principle of autosuggestion," said Napoleon Hill.

I started with an insight and ended up with sight; I have seen tangible results in my life such as an impeccable positive mindset, which is the reason I am writing this chapter. My baseline of positive attitude is fantastic, then super fantastic and finally super duper fantastic.

My contagious, positive attitude has given me beatitude at my job site, earning me the nickname FANTASTIC! I have seen colleagues who were less enthusiastic, and other employees who were moody brighten up and raise their level of happiness at least when we meet and communicate. This is the mirror neuron effect as described in positive psychology.

Begin with the outcome in mind. You have to see the project from start to finish by visualizing how the successful result will impact your life. Believe in the magic of believing before the process and see it manifest itself. Take a leap of faith forward into the unknown and see your undertaking bear fruit. If you believe it, it will work for you and vice versa.

Physicians have testified that patients who believe in their prescriptions see the best results.

You can use the following outline to try for yourself:

- Look for a serene place. For instance, take a notepad, flashlight, and pen into a closet.
- Jot down all thoughts that come to mind, both empowering and disempowering.
- Exhaust all thoughts until they begin to repeat themselves.
- Separate programs into group (A) – empowering; group (B) - disempowering.
- Transcribe into positive heading (A): rich, happy, healthy, lucky, generous, successful, likeable, intelligent, confident, strong proactive, good-humored, smiley, blessed, hardworking, attractive … and negative (B): poor, unhappy, sickly, wicket, bewitch, dishonest, stupid, weak,

unlucky, quarrelsome, hated, moody, greedy, unattractive, procrastinating, lazy, self-doubt.

Group B will dumbfound and daze you, but it is a crystal ball if harnessed. It will take you to the crest. It demands tremendous personal effort. When the daze is overwhelming, take a break but do not freak; resume after regaining sanity.

Negative programs also come from errors we committed in the past: unrealized dreams and aspirations, unforgiving and retributive attitude learned from unforgiving and avenging people around us, hatred of self/others, liking/love of self/others. The entire process is an ORDEAL: (Open, Right, Developmental, Enforcement, and Action (for) Life). It is the right action. Just be open and enforce it for your personal development. Eventually, your energy will lead to unstoppable synergy.

"You are the way you are because that's the way you want to be. If you wanted to be any different, you would be in the process of changing." said Fred Smith.

We are 100% in control of the process of decoding/re-encoding our subconscious and unleashing potential, just like we are in control of our attitude. The difference is that our negative programs might be influencing our attitude. Let's program our subconscious to work for us.

"The greatest discovery of my generation is that a human being can alter his life by altering his attitude." Said William James.

How can we reprogram the subconscious?

To be blind is bad, but worse is to have eyes and not see." said Helen Keller.

Synchronize the final process; fill the vacuum left by decoded negative programs with positive ones. It is the most difficult but groovy part of the process. Our burning desire to succeed will hone our power to alter the status quo, release our potential and unshackle us.

Unlike our minds, the subconscious works round the clock over our lifetime.

I came up with this formula to clear my path: Steadfast; Proactive; Assertive; Discipline and Emphatic (SPADE). I decided to pick up my SPADE and dig my goldmine. This metaphor propelled me to un-clutter my mind and get rid of the noise that held me back from moving forward. I apply SPADE in my daily activities.

SPADE forms the north arc; Action forms the south arc, meeting in the middle to form the circle of life. Diameter states: do it now; there is no tomorrow.

The Decoding and Reprogramming Process detailed here is systematic and has worked well for me:

- Understand the original cause of negative programs.
- What fuels programs?
- Negative programs are decoding support systems. (Is it the person, place, or thing?)
- Positive programs: supportive energy. (Is it the person, place or thing?)
- Use answers to handle corresponding situations promptly and assuredly.
- Note positive programs against negative ones.
- Example: rich > poor.
- Replace disempowering programs with corresponding empowering ones.
- Declare, affirm, meditate.
- Celebrate success and progress.
- Repeat process until corresponding positive programs replace negative ones.

I used the mirror technique created by Dr. Laura De Giorgio, a clinical hypnotherapist, in the decoding and encoding procedure. I look at myself squarely in the eyes in the mirror, build trust and bond with myself first. I encourage you to use this technique as well. Look in the mirror, ask self: am I poised for change? And be honest. The mirror reflects our image back to us, facilitates introspection, reaching into the subconscious to install our new software respecting our probing inquisitorial response/drive.

The mirror technique also helps translate our daily mantras, pep ourselves and prime our limitless possibilities. We have to Be, Do & Have respectively. Never try to Have, Be and then Do. Are we taking full advantage of our positive programs? Release their full potential. In the ORDEAL we will face obstacles, objections, mesmerisms, dilemmas… but our faith alone will resuscitate us.

I experienced a rollercoaster in some programs, and momentary crest falls in some. SPADE, daily meditations, declarations, and affirmations helped me get over most of them. Listen and watch motivational and inspirational tapes. Adjust or quit the relational illness environment that is holding you back and develop a nourishing mindset. READ (Rise Every day Above Death) & STUDY (Seek TuneUp Drive Yourself) consistently. Reading is the first step. Studying what you just read tunes you up, so you can apply yourself correctly through acquired knowledge; that is power!

You must take a conscious, meticulous approach to master your new positive programs through practice and exercise and unlearn the negative ones. The more engraved disempowering software was in your subconscious, the harder you have to work to reprogram it. For me, I revisited the reprogramming process several times, and I still do for the hard ones. I believe that the earlier in life one gets this awareness and uses this technique; the more reversible the situation. Once positive ones take root, you must practice and accentuate their benefits to prevent negative programs from resurfacing. The procedure is simple but not easy. Everyone can learn the art, apply the tact, earn the act, tell the facts and sell their story.

My first name is OLIVER (Open Life Invitation Earn Riches). I am inviting you to open up your life by giving reprogramming a chance because I am living proof that it works; this is not pontification. While in the process, I realized that I needed help, an accountability partner. Incidentally, my last name is ASAAH (Asking Seasoned Assistance Always Helps). That's how I decided to make my names acronyms and then put them in full to empower me in all my ventures.

We always need help from a loved supportive one who can hold us accountable and measure our progress, and reprimand us accordingly. It must be someone we trust and respect enough to bestow our life's purpose.

"Were it not for Tenzing the native guide, Edmund Hilary would not have made the historic climb of Mt. Everest." (John Maxwell 1984).

Do not frustrate yourself by expecting exquisite performance initially. Donald Trump's Apprentice became the number one reality show on NBC after several failures, but he chose to follow his instincts and not expert advice; hone your partner in crime for invincible results.

Everyone has empowering and disempowering programs. Just make sure the ratio greatly favors positive programs.

The reality is that 97 percent of the population works for three percent because our programming influences our choices. We can alter that equation by reprogramming our subconscious mind.

Biography

Being one of 24 siblings and having a Bachelor's in Law, Oliver Asaah has a powerful mélange of human relationships. He has several years of experience in network marketing in multiple companies. Oliver is a wellness entrepreneur building one of the biggest organizations in Genewize, a DNA customizing health, wellness & skincare solutions company. He is a speaker and mentor/coach who has a passion for motivating and inspiring people. Oliver has vested and harnessed the power of the subconscious through reprogramming and using his SPADE formula to maximize intuitive energy and synergy for personal and organizational achievement.

CONTACT INFORMATION

Oliver T. Asaah
Wealth Pool Industries
P O Box 1261
Greenbelt MD 20768
Phone: 301 537 2068
oliverasaah@yahoo.com

Chapter 17

THE JOURNEY OF SUCCESS

By Dr. Steven & Dr. Terresa Balestracci

Success is like a recipe; there are many ingredients. So, if there were a recipe for success, what would it be?

Well, perhaps the first step would be to have a dream, a reason, a why. Without this, it would be like going on a vacation without knowing where you are going.

Next, you need to have a plan or a vision. It would be the procedures to get to your destination. Some call it your roadmap.

After that, you would need the desire and passion to get you to your destination. We agree this would be your "fuel" to get you from point A to point B. This is vital to driving you toward your goal. Next, you need a support team or an accountability partner. This is very important so that you have people to encourage you along the way. This will assist you in overcoming the challenges that you will undoubtedly face.

You may not always have control over some of the challenges that you will face along your journey, but two things you can control are your thoughts and with whom you surround yourself. Achieving success is not easy, but surrounding yourself with people who believe in you, and support and encourage you will accelerate the speed at which you can reach success. This would also include reading books that inspire you to succeed and grow as a person.

Finally, the last step would be to celebrate! When you achieve your goals and dreams and every win along the way, you should rejoice and be thankful for the many blessings that you have.

We believe that a key ingredient to achieving success at any level is having faith, not only in ourselves but most of all, having faith in God. We believe that God puts dreams in our minds and hope in our hearts for a reason. He truly wants us to have the many blessings that he has to offer. We are truly thankful for the dreams and desires that the Lord has placed in our hearts and minds, and the daily courage He graces us with to live them out.

Placed in my heart and the daily courage He graces me with to live them out!

Our favorite quote on success is by George Sheehan which states, "Success means having the courage, the determination and the will to become the person you believe you were meant to be."

We love this quote because it is also the true meaning of success. Nowhere in the quote does it talk about how much money you make or how many material objects you possess. This quote can truly be applied to any person and any situation.

Without courage, you allow fear to prevent you from taking the next step that is vital to achieving success. Without determination, you allow challenges to prevent you from continuing on your path to achieving success.

One of the major challenges that we believe holds people back from achieving success is fear. Overcoming fear is one the most difficult things to do, but if a person does not overcome a fear that is a roadblock to achieving their goals, they will never achieve success associated with that goal or dream.

We believe that any super-successful person has had to overcome many fears and obstacles on their journey to success. And, by pushing through, you will grow as a person and be another step closer to achieving success.

An analogy that we can apply is that of a small child who is trying to walk. First, the child has to have the courage to take the first step and even after they try and try and fall many times, which represents the challenges, they must keep going, or they will never succeed in walking. If this child were to allow their fear of falling to get in the way, they would never even try again.

This is why we believe that it is an innate instinct for us to want to achieve. It is up to us whether we are going to allow the challenges that we face on our journey of success to strengthen us or weaken us. This is simply a decision that we must make that will allow us to turn our challenges into strengths.

To us, success is pursuing your dreams and goals despite the challenges that may occur during the process. We have had many challenges in our businesses and personal lives.

Whether it is a two-month delay in the build-out of our office space, an employee that has stolen from us, one of our kids getting sick, or losing a loved one, we have faced these challenges and never lost sight of our dreams and goals. What we have realized as we have grown over the years through our experiences and education is that the challenges never stop coming, but how we react to them has changed. For example, a situation that five years ago would have distracted us and taken us off the path to our goals for weeks or months, now only lasts for hours or days.

A mindset that we have learned to draw upon is to improvise, adapt and overcome which has allowed us to open our minds and understand that our minds are extremely powerful, so powerful that it brings to mind other quotes we continue to draw upon and try to impress upon others to do the same.

Just a few of these are:

"Whatever the mind can conceive, it can achieve!" and as Henry Ford has said "Whether you think you can or you think you can't…You're right." Something that Yoda said in the Star Wars series, "There is no try, there is only do or not do." Lastly, an important concept that we teach our kids, "Never let anyone's opinion of you become your reality unless it is a Positive opinion!"

We believe the greatest tip we have learned in life and business is forgiveness and being able to leave the past in the past. Not only is it vital to forgive others when they have wronged you, but it is just as important, to forgive yourself.

Not forgiving yourself can destroy your self-worth. And, it can send you down a path of self-destruction and mediocrity. It has happened to us many times in our lives where we were presented with challenges, things that hurt us financially and emotionally, and we dwelled on them and allowed them to steal happiness from our lives and enthusiasm from our spirits.

We have personally seen people in our personal and professional lives who carry baggage from the past and allow it to destroy their lives. They wind up getting ill, mentally and physically and prevent any chance of happiness and success they ever had.

Because of the personal growth and development training that we have experienced, we realized how much they held us back, and delayed and distracted us from our goals and dreams in the pursuit of our success.

We believe that some of the most important keys to achieving success are having desire and passion. We both grew up in Italian-American households where there was a great deal of influence from family members.

Food was always present no matter what the occasion or lack of occasion. The main thing about this combination of family, food, and conversation was passion and desire. These people were very passionate and expressive, to say the least, about what seemed like everything they spoke of, regardless of whether it was a sporting event, last night's dinner or a day at "work."

The majority of them desired to be more successful than the last generation, as was the last generation's desire for them. This love of life and people was a driving force in their pursuit of happiness and success, and has influenced us and helped to define who we are today.

Other major influences that have impacted our lives are our role models and mentors. While we learned from many authors, speakers, and educators, we do have a few favorites.

Two of our favorite role models are B.J. Palmer, developer of chiropractic and world-renowned educator and entrepreneur, and Warren Buffet, world-renowned entrepreneur, and business mogul. They represent success achieved through passion, desire, and vision.

Two of our favorite mentors are Marc Accetta, world-renowned trainer, speaker, and entrepreneur, and Matt Morris, world-renowned best-selling author, speaker, and entrepreneur. Marc and Matt are both incredibly successful people who have taught us so much about life and helped us achieve our current level of success through their guidance, incredible leadership and training. They are passionate about teaching people to achieve the success that they have, which is a quality that we greatly admire.

The thing that we are most passionate about is helping people. This is why we pursued our careers in chiropractic. We feel that chiropractic can positively impact people's lives more profoundly since we, as doctors/teachers, empower people to take a more active role in their health and well-being rather than being victims and passively existing through the symptom-based system that the current healthcare model offers.

We also have passion and desire to help people through our other business in the industry of network marketing and travel. It is with this business that we have learned personal growth and development skills, as well as the skills to create additional streams of income and be able to assist others to achieve the same. As we experience wins in our businesses by helping people, we achieve spiritual and emotional wins for ourselves. This is the satisfaction that continues to motivate us to keep going in our pursuit of success.

Another desire we have as we continue to pursue our dreams is that we make our children proud of us. We believe that the best way we can do this is to live with passion, have the courage to finish what we start and lead by example.

We try to be as mindful of this as possible as we raise our three children. We want them to have their own dreams, and we do not want to live vicariously through them and prevent them from reaching their full potential. Also, we remind them that even when they have a class or subject that they do not have much interest in that they should put forth the effort, because they might just be surprised at the outcome, especially about the growth of self-confidence and self-worth.

When we were growing up, we always had the desire for our parents to be proud of us; however, now that we have kids, they are who we most want to make proud. We feel that achieving this would be one of the greatest successes in our lives.

As parents and successful business owners, we believe that you have to lead by example. Whether you see yourself as a leader or not, many of us are viewed that way because of the actions that we take and the way that we inspire the people around us. Leadership is a combination of many qualities that an individual must possess.

A true leader is someone who can motivate people to take action through communication and representation as well as having the ability to overcome resistance to challenges to attain a common goal for the betterment of both the individual and the team. A great leader, Zig Ziglar, once said, "If you help enough other people get what they want, you get what you want."

Finally, for us, we have realized that success in a culmination of many components with some of the main ones being faith, vision, passion, desire, belief, courage, resilience, attitude, humbleness, integrity, honor, purpose, leadership, knowledge and the application of knowledge.

We are truly blessed and humbled to have the opportunity to share some of our thoughts on success to positively impact the lives of others with the hopes that this will assist them on their journey of success.

Biography

Dr. Steven & Dr. Terresa Balestracci met in Davenport, Iowa, while attending Palmer College of Chiropractic where they both graduated with Doctor of Chiropractic degrees. They have owned a successful chiropractic office in Bridgewater, New Jersey, for over 15 years. They have been involved in network marketing with a company called WorldVentures where they rank in the top 1% of the company's independent representatives. Michael, Gianna, and Cristian, their three children, inspire them to strive to achieve higher levels of success and for whom they desire to leave a legacy.

Contact Information

Dr. Steven & Dr. Terresa Balestracci
Phone: 484-375-5380 / 484-375-5385
Address: 2385 Silvano Dr., Macungie, PA 18062

Chapter 18

ESSENTIAL SUCCESS: "A LIVING TRANSFORMATION"

By Ray Blanchard, Ph.D.

If you knew you only had a short time to live, and then it's going to be over, what would you do with the rest of your life?

This message is for individuals who desire to succeed beyond measure and who are urgent to live their true potential. That means living with purpose and passion. That means having the courage to dream big and to go after what you want like the present is all you have. In this crash course on self-transformation, several basic understandings and distinctions are shared so you can flip the switch to your success. It will be the reader's challenge to live such wisdom and to keep those distinctions alive.

My story may be like yours, a typical "zero to hero" scenario. It reveals lessons for a clear path to change lives for the better. It is amazing how these humble beginnings built such a solid foundation for the achievements that followed.

I am one of 12 children, born to a strong-willed Mississippi farmer. I am the youngest of six sons. My mother always stressed learning from your hardships and moving on without complaining and giving something to your neighbors along the way. Life was a struggle for my parents, always barely making ends meet. Finally, when I was about 12 years old, the ravages of a tornado tearing through the little shotgun house we lived in forced us to pick up and leave the farm my father worked since he was born some 66 years earlier. I had been a "smart" little kid in the country school where my aunt was the principal, and most of the grades were in the same room.

But, moving to the big city in St. Louis, I was quite unprepared to compete with my classmates initially. Not liking that, I worked hard to prove myself, to help the family out and make my parents proud. I got a job in a grocery store and ran a newspaper route. I paid for my clothes and school supplies. By the second year in high school, I was able to start sports, where I learned to strive even harder and always aim to win. By taking a new job in the morning before school at the local hospital and running two miles through the park to make it to morning classes, I became a good athlete and student. My counselors took notice of my efforts and decided to help me get into college since my parents would not have been able to help me at all. Forging ahead with encouragement from my advisor, I finally got a break. I went to night school at Washington University in St. Louis until I earned the opportunity to go full time. One professor took a special interest in me, after noticing my love for classical philosophy, and helped me to get two degrees and a fellowship to a doctoral program where I excelled.

Two key mentors pushed and goaded me to keep moving until I graduated to become a Doctor of Philosophy in Psychology after a little more than three years. My proudest moment was when my mom was able to come 2,000 miles on her first airplane flight to see the first of her brood get an advanced college degree. Since then, other mentors at significant stages of my life helped me go to the next level of success, through the wisdom they had gained and imparted to me. The unbelievable support from these life coaches has taken me around the world in more ways than one and has stewarded me to extraordinary accomplishments and joy. I feel blessed and grateful, and I live with the passion for giving back.

The greatest success lesson in all my experiences is to *"always believe,"* especially when the light is dim, and there doesn't seem to be a way out. Keep your belief strong and determined to outlast the challenges. Don't ever give up on what matters. You often gain the victory in the darkest hour, by that one extra heave or burst of effort like your life depended on it. In the race for life, it's that last act that gives you victory or marks the final arrival of a long journey.

The completion of a heartfelt commitment is the ultimate arrival. But, it is the process of getting there with joy and passion that is the best and most meaningful. If you can live your life with joy and ease while attaining satisfaction in personal, professional and spiritual affairs, you are a success.

On your way to the top, it is important to give back and help someone else. *"Reach back and pull someone else up."* Pay it forward. This is both satisfaction for you, and it makes a difference in the social consciousness of the world. These are the yin and yang of a principled life, and the most important character traits in achieving complete success – getting results and being a giver.

Four key factors are always present in my successes and are most often in those giants we revere as well: (1) hard work, (2) knowledge, (3) attitude and (4) love of God or the Almighty.

Hard Work

Let's face it - life can be tough. Not many successes have been authentically achieved without hard work. That does not mean that life has to be hard. It just means be prepared and go the extra mile. Make it a practice.

For instance, if you are exercising, do a few more minutes or add a few extra repetitions. It is well established that the greatest consistent results come from the extra efforts rather than the easy actions with which you start.

In relationships, you should stretch yourself and have a few more authentic conversations with loved ones and colleagues each week. You will quickly realize that you have super-powered your network of support. Support is vital to being the best you can be and to giving peak performances. Plus, you tend to open up a lot more opportunities and possibilities, personally and professionally, because you reached out.

Refrain from having to be "right" in every conversation. "Being Right" is a social disease and an addiction that destroys relationships on all levels. At least two or three times a week, be conscious of your impulse to dig in your heels to argue your point. Then "let it go." Create win-win interactions and experiences that will uplift your friendships and open more space for everyone to grow. All will be happier and healthier for it, and it is widely believed to add a few more years to your life as well.

These acts may take more focused awareness of your relationships, but the rewards are worth it in terms of your experience of success. You shape the consciousness landscape that surrounds you and enhance your social capital among your peers.

Also, invest a few hours a week in personal growth and inner development activities. The value you gain accumulates and even compounds. By the end of a month, you will notice a big difference. By the end of a year, you will have put in almost a week's investment into yourself. Remember that, after your maker, YOU are the ANSWER and the key to your success.

I strongly suggest pursuing effective empowerment seminars as well. You can learn more about yourself sometimes from such outside sources than you can ever learn from your already existing views of life. I had a true "enlightenment experience" in a seminar in the early years of my professional life, which was life-altering. I treasure it to this day. It could be like that for you, too.

Knowledge

Knowledge is the key to power. And, power is the ability to turn possibility into reality. The first principle of knowledge is to "know thyself." To accomplish that, one needs to examine his life and see what makes himself tick thoroughly. Sorting through your past experiences and beliefs can tell you why you feel, think and do what you do, and why you get the results you get. Realizing this gives you access to your life script and behavior patterns at the root level, thereby allowing you to create a new map or blueprint for success.

You should practice going into deep thought a few minutes a day to specifically examine the genesis of various beliefs you have, and make corrections that would lead to more expertise, free choice and precise actions that create the results you want. Learn to use the "stop-look-listen" process for self-reflection and life improvement. Stop being on auto-pilot and reactive behavior. Look at life from a new angle or perspective. Listen to your heartfelt commitment rather than negative self-talk. This will help you to make strides toward your higher goals steadily.

Also, take time to reflect on the material you read each day, and examine it from different angles and understandings. Don't be a "yes" machine. Challenge ideas. This is a practice in discipline and critical analysis, which enriches your creativity and ability to invent new possibilities.

You should dedicate an extra two hours a week focusing on a hobby. It will keep you fresh and will likely play a part in the rest of your career, by adding richness and a new dimension to whatever you do. The added time per year that you put into your deeper interests and career will put you heads and shoulders above your peers and will give you the competitive edge to increase your chances for greatness.

Attitude

All reality is dictated by the context that supports it. Positive thoughts lead to positive attitude and actions, and negative ones lead to negative outcomes. In effect, thoughts are things. It would be prudent to deliberately train your attitude and thought processes to generate your desire. This is the key to flipping the switch to success.

Several years ago, one of my good friends who had a less-than-pleasant attitude came to this realization and did something about it, and it significantly shifted his business. He made a paradigm shift to accentuate the positive and eliminate the negative. He started a slogan for his company and followed it: *"I shall not complain."*

He made it a point to eliminate at least a few complaints a day, noting each time he interrupted his negative thoughts. The impact of eliminating several hundred negative imprints a year altered his outlook and ultimately created more customers. Consider doing the same exercise for a year. Include thoughts about your job, family, neighbor, the weather, love life, bank account, the economy, friends, etc. *"You reap what you sow."* Change your mind and change your life.

Love of God or the Almighty

The human condition is the continuous search for meaning and fulfillment. This usually brings up our spiritual reality, what sustains us and supports our reason for being.

Truth and meaning are a matter of interpretation. We are continuously interpreting and assessing our spiritual reality, making meaning out of it, and using our interpretations and meanings to act in ways we think would fulfill our lives.

Regardless of how one arrives at their conclusion, the majority of well-known great achievers indicate that material success alone is meaningless, and success without having a sense of fulfilling a higher purpose is emptiness.

Some people, for instance, interpret that there is a greater source of life and meaning outside of our own interpretation, and it is our pleasure to serve It. Some do not. We get to choose for ourselves, which is true for us. Our happiness and motivation often depend on it. For me, the Almighty source of life and meaning is God.

The pursuit of meaning or truth is a very personal and private matter. The sooner you begin the quest, it is to your advantage. Regardless of what you discover, the act of giving and making a difference through service seems to be on the right path to finding out. It provides the most empowering sense of purpose and deep satisfaction that propels us to achieve.

Contributing to world transformation and peace are popular undertakings. Healing the environment, ending hunger on the planet or providing health needs to the sick are also possibilities. Serving your community, church or charity are other ways to quell the thirst. Contributing a few hours of service a week will culminate in several weeks a year of giving to others and making a difference. It makes you feel good about yourself. It is life-redeeming, and it powerfully affects your sense of value.

Success is determined by how well you live your life. Wealth, character or a combination thereof, are the measures. The defining factors include: the risks you take, the courage you demonstrate, the ease in letting go of disappointment and pain, the ability to shift your points of view and come off "autopilot," the ability to think and create possibility in the face of the impossible, how you include people and bring them forward, the patience and love expressed and received, and the difference you make in the lives of others.

Leaders possess these qualities in abundance, and in sharing them, they make the difference between potential and reality. *"Having what it takes and not using it is a waste, but living such qualities can transform the world."*

Success is self-realization. Being real and being oneself is the most one can be. Our challenge is to strive for such completeness so that we reach the pinnacle of human achievement and excellence. My favorite quote, *"To thine own self, be true,"* captures it succinctly.

The way of the Buddha is an exquisite example. It is the way of ease, where effort and effortlessness are balanced in perfect harmony. It demonstrates integrity, which is *Essential Success*. The life of Jesus is a perfect model of success in action, handling challenges and relating to others. He is an example of acceptance and inclusion, never giving up, purpose and passion, and overcoming while still loving - *A Living Transformation*. Together they represent our ultimate goal, which is to be whole, perfect and complete. And that is *Essential Success: A Living Transformation*.

BIOGRAPHY

Dr. Ray Blanchard, the founder of Blanchard Consulting Group, is a seasoned entrepreneur, consultant, and media producer. He earned his Ph.D. from the University of Oregon and garnered praise for his films *THE ANSWER To Absolutely Everything* and the *FIRESIDE FORUM*. With more than 100,000 client-graduates worldwide, he was elected to the esteemed *Transformational Leadership Council.*

CONTACT INFORMATION

Dr. Ray Blanchard
youcountnow@gmail.com
541-912-8571
www.rayblanchard.com

CHAPTER 19

REACHING SUCCESS WITH EXCELLENCE

By Ellen Reid

It seems like every day I wake up, and there's something new and different about my industry. And I don't mean some little change; I'm talking about something earthshaking, life-changing, revolutionary.

Okay, maybe it's not every day. However, it started a few years ago, and the momentum is most definitely building. I work in the publishing industry, specifically the self-publishing end of it. I've been involved in this exciting field since 1998, and I have seen what feels like a century's worth of changes take place in just over a decade. These include things like digital printing, print on demand, and, most recently, e-books and readers.

However, one thing I have observed to be constant is that those authors and books that have been successful – and in fact, people who are successful in any area of endeavor, whether business or personal life – are those that demonstrate excellence. I have made excellence the cornerstone of my success.

"Excellence" has become my mantra, my branding, and my way of life. I'm not saying that excellence will guarantee success. However, I can't imagine real success without excellence being a part of it.

I wouldn't say excellence has always been a part of my life. However, it is something that was tempered in the fires of my life's adventures. My father was of the narcissistic persuasion, so no matter what I accomplished it somehow became about him. I soon learned that he demanded perfection, which, even to this day, I don't believe is possible. However, I was continually striving to do better and better. I may have missed perfection, but I guarantee you, I developed a real track record of excellence.

As I grew and matured, pursuing studies in personal growth, I came to learn how to transform my feelings of frustration with my father's unattainable demands into positive motivation to excel. Whether it was in my first career in sales and marketing, where I rose up the ranks to international buyer, frequently being sent to Asia to develop products, or my current consulting/book shepherding career, in which I have been acknowledged Beverly Hills' Premier Book Consultant, I found myself compelled to both produce excellence and encourage others to it.

Excellence is an interesting concept. People know it when they see it, but they may not know *why* they recognize something as excellent.

In my work, there are certain definite guidelines for what excellence is not. For example, typos in a book are a sure sign of less than excellent work – and this erodes the value of the message. So, for me, one major element of excellence is attention to detail.

That can be reflected by a well-proofread galley, which is pretty evident to everyone. But, it can also be reflected in subtle things like the amount of space between lines on a page (called leading – which is a term taken for the days of hand-setting type with individual letters cast from metal, like lead, and adding a line of lead in between the lines) or the amount of space between letters, called kerning. (I have no idea why they call it that.)

Another thing – one of those changes I was talking about – is that computers instill a false sense of ability. Anyone with a computer and Microsoft Word can create what may look like an actual book. But it's not, which you can tell when you compare a page done in Word with a page done by a professional with a page layout program. This leads me to another big tip: Know when you can handle something yourself and know when it will serve you to bring in a professional.

When it comes to excellence, professionals are worth their weight in platinum. What I have observed is that some people are great at some aspects of their work, mediocre at other aspects and downright poor at others. So, one key I've found for myself and that I share with clients is to evaluate what's necessary for any task and determine which you can legitimately do yourself and which you need help to do.

I counsel people to be ruthless with themselves and not be afraid to admit there are just some things they're not great at doing. While there may be some subtle message in our culture that says we're supposed to be able to do everything ourselves, in my experience, it's the very rare person who can do it all with excellence.

With writers, the things they need to look at include the actual writing of their book. Even the biggest names in the business, authors who have made millions and published lots of books, will tell you that one of their greatest assets and allies is their editor. While you may not be an author, you most likely do write letters for your business. Make sure they are well proofed, if possible by someone other than you. Catch all the typos, make sure it looks good on the page, neither too high or too low on your letterhead. Make sure your point is stated and what you are asking the recipient to do is specific.

Okay, I know you may not send a lot of letters, but I'll bet you send several emails each day. While some of the ideas above may not apply, do proofread your emails for typos and grammar. And make sure what you're saying is clear.

Back to my writing clients. Not only do they need to start by making sure their manuscript is in excellent shape, but they also need to have a powerful cover. This means they need to get a book cover designer, not the daughter of a friend of theirs who did very well in her college design class. Book design is a specialized field and not every good graphic designer knows the ins & outs of book cover design. Ditto interior design. You would be amazed at the difference in readability when a good interior book designer gets hold of a manuscript.

Presumably, you can translate what I'm saying here to your own life and business. If you are putting something out that represents you or your business – and I mean anything from a wedding invitation to a printed brochure – make sure it's done right, by a professional if necessary, if you want it to reflect excellence. And do your homework; if you're looking for a professional, don't just pick the first name that comes up when you google graphic designer. Part of excellence is following up with samples of work and references from others who have used the person's services.

Another area that comes up for my clients is promotional writing. On books, that's everything from the title and subtitle, to the back cover and the short author's bio. What I often have to communicate with my clients is that just because they can write an excellent book does not mean they can write the text that is needed to sell their masterpiece. Again, it's a matter of finding a professional who can articulate what you're offering in a way that potential customers will recognize it as having value to them. My experience is that many – maybe most – people are so close to their message, product, or service, that they want to tell everyone about all of it. A good promotional copywriter will be able to advise on how much needs to be said to generate interest, and how much is so much information that you lose interest.

Bottom line, what I preach and what I practice is that the right resource people – those who demonstrate excellence – will contribute to my excellence. And that contributes to my success.

Which brings me to the question, what is success?. When I was younger, I thought success was easy to measure. It had to do with how much money you made. Then, after I had made a fair amount of money, I discovered that I didn't feel particularly successful.

So, I began exploring success from the inside out, which involved things like spirituality and personal growth. Those explorations revealed many avenues that I am still considering and dealing with myself. This is a lot like peeling away layers of an onion in that there's always another layer to work through. I expect these pursuits to be ongoing pretty much as long as I've got a body and am here on this earth.

In the end, it was probably this inner questing that brought my awareness to excellence. I find that to have genuine satisfaction in my life, I not only need to have balance in my life but I also need to make sure that I am feeling fulfilled by what I am doing. I am driven to do excellent work and to have my work reflect the excellence of who I am– and, in a very real sense the excellence of who we all are. I find great satisfaction in encouraging my clients to be more of who they can be.

I can't tell you how great it feels to hear how thrilled a client is when they receive their book from the printer and hold it in their hands for the first time. In virtually every case, they tell me that it's far beyond what they had ever envisioned. They feel great, and I feel good because I know they have achieved something they can be very proud of – because it reflects excellence.

BIOGRAPHY

Ellen Reid is a Book Shepherd extraordinaire. Since 1998 she has been assisting authors in exceeding their dreams for an outstanding book they can be proud of, and that stands up to any competition. Acknowledged as Beverly Hills' Premier Book Consultant, Ellen has built her career on excellence. She is the author of the award-winning *Putting Your Best Book Forward; A book shepherd's secrets for creating award-winning books that sell*.

CONTACT INFORMATION

Ellen Reid
Book Shephard
(310) 862-2573
ellen@bookshep.com

Chapter 20

BECOMING THE MAN IN THE ARENA

By Mikel Erdman

I grew up on a farm in southwestern Oregon, in a very small town named Bandon. It's famous now because a rich guy from Chicago came and built some of the top-rated golf courses in the world there. When I was growing up, it was nothing like that. It was a sleepy coastal town surviving on the final feast of the logging and fishing industries and very little else.

My dad was in the meat business just like his father before him, and his grandfather before him. In the summers, we fished our commercial salmon troller for Chinook and Coho salmon and occasionally took off after albacore tuna if they came close enough to the shore. Working these businesses meant long hours and sore muscles and a lot of ingenuity and resourcefulness to stay afloat.

I was surrounded by hard work while growing up, the kind of work that they would feature on the television show "Dirty Jobs." In fact, these were the type of jobs that you had to have a whole different set of clothes for work than you'd ever wear for anything else. It was next to impossible to get the smells out once you've worn them around the feedlot or in the back end of the boat with diesel fumes, fish innards, and cow manure.

From as early as I can remember, I was doing chores and participating in the family businesses. Believe it or not, just growing up in that small business, the do-it-yourself atmosphere had a lot to do with me achieving a high level of success in my life. I learned a whole lot of lessons about dealing with adversity and rising to the challenge.

I saw the magic of new ideas formulated in my mind and then brought to reality by the power of vision, dedication, and persistence. And I learned one of the most important lessons about success right there in the middle of those hard, dirty jobs – that not all good ideas work out and true success comes to those who are willing to face their failures and step out once again to achieve their dreams.

In fact, if you look at some of the most successful people in the world, their careers never shoot to the top without any challenges or setbacks along the way. Some of the most respected and revered leaders in our land seemed to be just a long string of failures accentuated by moments of greatness and characterized by the unwillingness to give up or give in.

Take this person for example:

He was born into poverty and early in his life, his family was broke and were forced out of their home. He had to work as a child to support them. His mother passed away when he was only nine years old. By 22, he had started and failed in his own business. Shortly after that, he ran for public office and lost, then started a second business which failed within two years, on borrowed money. A few years later, his fiancée died unexpectedly, and he suffered a complete nervous breakdown. Throughout his life, he lost eight separate elections, but in 1860, he was finally elected President of the United States of America. Who was he? Mr. Abraham Lincoln.

There is no question that Abraham Lincoln is one of the most revered leaders in all of American history. When you look at the record of his life, however, you'd be hard-pressed to believe in his greatness, up until the point that he successfully led his country through one of the most critical periods of its existence. What if he had given up? What if he had quit after his first business failed?

It's clear that Mr. Lincoln's failures did not define the altitude of his achievement. And this point is true for you too! It's one of the hardest lessons to learn and is critical to your success in life. You have the power to change. You have the power to make course corrections throughout your life and learn from the challenges that you encounter along your journey. You and only you can permit yourself to use that wisdom to move forward and make your mark on the world.

Growing up in an entrepreneurial environment and seeing this cycle of success and failure play out has led me to understand that it isn't a single defeat that can cause you to lose the game of life. Your success is based on your willingness to get up off the ground, dust yourself off and get yourself back in the game. You must understand that it's just part of the process and isn't unique to you.

In my own life, I've had to overcome a few colossal failures. I once started a real estate advertising technology firm that took off like a rocket ship. We had developed a novel new technology product that made a lot of sense in the marketplace and added a lot of value to the businesses of real estate agents, mortgage lenders and other real estate professionals who used our systems. We grew the company from zero, with no outside investment, to over 1 million dollars in sales and from 2 to 35 employees within 18 months. I thought we'd hit the big one, and I was only 33 years old at the time.

It felt like that entrepreneurial dream had come true. There were a lot of expenses, but the cash-flow was great, and it looked like we had made it! In fact, this was the first time in my life that I knew what it meant to have no money troubles at all. We were completely debt-free outside of the home and had plenty of reserves stashed away. We had more money than we knew what to do with it.

I wish I could tell you that the fairy tale lasted, the business continued to grow, and we rode off into the sunset with our bags of riches. It didn't. In the second winter, the business changed fast. The technology that our business was based on completely revolutionized within the two years we were in business and made a large part of what we delivered irrelevant. And the employees and overhead didn't slow down at the same rate as the revenue coming in.

They say that the larger a ship is, the longer it takes to slow it down or change its course. That is true in business. All of the sales revenue that we made in the run-up of the company had been reinvested, and the overhead started to eat us alive. We ended up closing the company at the three-year mark with hundreds of thousands of dollars of our personal investment lost.

Let me tell you something that hurt. I mean it physically hurt. I was crushed. I had poured three years of my life working up to 16 hours a day to make this dream come true. I had a serious case of self-doubt that I could ever make anything successful again. I mean, if you had something so powerful that took off so fast and made so much money while doing an incredible amount of good in the world and you lost it all, wouldn't you question your ability to make it happen again?

It took a couple of months to start feeling better after that failure, but the resilience that I learned back on the farm showed up, and I set my sights on the next chapter of my life. I got busy and came up with a new plan. I set out to reinvent myself. I had to pull myself and my family out of this financial wasteland. I went on over the next three years to have the highest personal income years in my entire career.

What would have happened if I'd just given up? Sure, I had a lot of reasons to lie on the couch and throw a big pity party. A lot of people would have understood why I wasn't achieving anything after seeing that huge "swing-and-a-miss." In fact, I had a few of them telling me that maybe I should just lie low, you know, get a safe and secure job and give up on those big dreams. But I knew, deep down in my heart, that the failure of that one business couldn't define who I was in the world and the value that I could continue to bring people in so many ways.

It's the same way for you too! No matter what trials and tribulations you've faced on your journey thus far, you can decide right here and now that you're going on to bigger and better things. You can set your sights on the pinnacle of your achievement and with commitment, hard work, and persistence, you can make those dreams turn into reality.

Most importantly, I want every one of you to know that you have everything it takes to achieve your goals. You have been given the most powerful computer, a sound operating system, and the most incredible architecture ever known on the face of the Earth since the day you were created. It's up to you to harness that power and make a decision to accomplish your goals.

Recently, as we were celebrating the New Year and looking forward to the great events and successes to come in the year ahead, I had a startling and somewhat chilling revelation. This was not just a new year; this was a new decade. A new decade! I realized that at the end of this decade, I would be nearing 50 years old, my children would be most of the way through their school years and off to college, and I would have come upon the time in my life that I had always dreamed of, being retired early and traveling the world. I gulped hard and felt my hands get a little clammy.

I got just a little bit anxious about what I would accomplish, starting off into this new era of my life. There have been many times in my life that I was in this same position. It seems like the nervousness never quite goes away. That familiar dark, burning feeling in the pit of my stomach that begs the question "Mikel, are you up to the challenge?"

I made a decision right then that this decade would be the most productive era of my life and I would dedicate myself to plan and execute better than ever before. You see, that has been one of the most critical secrets to my success, and it's the same with every other successful person that I've ever met, listened to, or read about. The willingness to take the uneasiness and uncertainty of challenging circumstances and face them head-on is a hallmark of a true leader.

Napoleon Hill, one of the greatest thought leaders who ever lived, said it best "Whatever the mind can conceive and believe, the mind can achieve."

James Nesmith had a dream of improving his golf game – and he developed a unique method of achieving his goal. Until he devised this method, he was just your average weekend golfer, shooting in mid- to low-nineties. Then, for seven years, he completely quit the game. He never touched a club. He never set foot on a fairway.

Ironically, it was during this seven-year break from the game that he came up with his amazingly effective technique for improving his game – a technique we can all learn from. In fact, the first time he set foot on a golf course after his hiatus from the game, he shot an astonishing 74! He cut 20 strokes off his average without having swung a golf club in seven years! Unbelievable! Not only that, but his physical condition had deteriorated during those seven years.

What was his secret? Visualization. You see, Major Nesmith had spent those seven years as a prisoner of war in North Vietnam. During those seven years, he was imprisoned in a cage that was approximately four and one-half feet high and five feet long.

During almost the entire time, he was imprisoned, he saw no one, talked to no one and experienced no physical activity. During the first few months, he did virtually nothing but hope and prayed for his release. Then he realized he had to find some way to occupy his mind or he would lose his sanity and probably his life. That's when he learned the power of building his future in his mind's eye.

In his mind, he selected his favorite golf course and started playing golf. Every day, he played a full 18 holes at the legendary country club of his dreams. He experienced everything to the last detail. He saw himself dressed in his golfing clothes. He smelled the fragrance of the trees and the freshly trimmed grass. He experienced different weather conditions – windy spring days, overcast winter days, and sunny summer mornings.

In his imagination, every detail, the individual blades of grass, the trees, the singing birds, the scampering squirrels and the lay of the course became real.

He felt the grip of the club in his hands. He instructed himself as he practiced smoothing out his down-swing and the follow-through on his shot. Then he watched the ball arc down the exact center of the fairway, bounce a couple of times and roll to the exact spot he had selected, all in his mind.

In the real world, he was in no hurry. He had no place to go. So, in his mind, he took every step on his way to the ball, just as if he was physically on the course. It took him just as long as the imaginary time to play 18 holes as it would have taken in reality. Not a detail was omitted. Not once did he ever miss a shot, never a hook or a slice, never a missed putt.

Eighteen holes of golf every day, seven days a week for seven years. Twenty strokes off his score for a lifetime best score of 74.

Here is the question for all of us as we start our new decade:

What are you visualizing?

What do you have your mind focused on and where is that focus taking you?

Without a clear vision of where you are going, you're likely to get lost along the way. You may end up looking back at the beginning of 2020 wondering which road you took and how you arrived where you are.

It's your choice. It all comes down to a few simple planning steps and committed action on a daily basis in the direction of your dreams.

1. Fix in your mind the exact goal or desire in your life.
2. Determine exactly what you intend to give in return for the achievement of your goal.
3. Establish a definite date for the achievement of the goal.
4. Create a definite plan for carrying out your desire and begin at once, whether you are ready or not, to put this plan into action
5. Write a clear and concise statement including the exact goal, what you intend to give in return, the time limit for

its achievement and the plan through which you intend to succeed.
6. Read your written statement aloud for a minimum of twice daily, once immediately after arising in the morning, and once again immediately before retiring at night.

In closing, I'd like to leave you with two comments. The first of these is that your failures don't define you and can't defeat you unless you let them. Failure is simply a reflection point on your way to your ultimate destination. Failures are an opportunity to learn what to do better next time and to develop the wisdom that you'll need to impact the lives of many in a positive way.

Lastly, I want you to know that taking a step into the unknown on faith is purely courageous. If you have a desire to become more in the world, if you have a song in your heart that has not been released to the wind, if you have a blessing inside of you waiting to burst out showing your greatness to the world, then get moving. Don't waste a single moment worrying about what might happen if you fail. Do everything in your power to avoid failure but accept setbacks as part of the process of achieving your dreams.

And finally, a favorite quote from one of our cherished American leaders, Teddy Roosevelt, who reminds us that the person of action and determination is to be admired:

"It is not the critic who counts; not the man who points out how the strong man stumbles, or where the doer of deeds could have done them better. The credit belongs to the man who is actually in the arena, whose face is marred by dust and sweat and blood; who strives valiantly; who errs, who comes short again and again, because there is no effort without error and shortcoming; but who does actually strive to do the deeds; who knows great enthusiasms, the great devotions; who spends himself in a worthy cause; who at the best knows in the end the triumph of high achievement, and who at the worst, if he fails, at least fails while daring greatly, so that his place shall never be with those cold and timid souls who neither know victory nor defeat."

Biography

Mikel Erdman has been engaging and inspiring sales and marketing professionals for more than 15 years. A product of the success principles he teaches, Mikel started his entrepreneurial career immediately after graduating from college. He became a self-made millionaire at the age of 30. He has successfully started and grown multiple companies in the mortgage, technology, and advertising arenas.

Contact Information

Mikel Erdman
Goodyear, Arizona
(360) 450-3551
http://www.mikelerdman.com

Chapter 21

INSPIRATION WHEN YOU LEAST EXPECT IT

By Brian Mahany

There is a picture on my refrigerator, a picture of a little boy. He is a little boy that I have never met, a boy with a bright smile even though he is suffering from an extremely rare and deadly cancer. Why is this picture on my refrigerator? Hopefully, by the end of this story, you will know the answer.

Although I have a large and beautiful home office, I frequently set up my laptop in the kitchen and work there. For many people, the kitchen is the "center" of their home. Across from the kitchen table stands the refrigerator. Like most other homes, our refrigerator does more than just keep food cold; it also serves as a message center and a place to display pictures, artwork, and magnets from trips taken long ago.

There are four pictures on my refrigerator. A Christmas family photo sent by a friend, one of my long-ago deceased family pet mastiff named Bear, a picture of my late father taken during World War II, and one of the little boy whose name I do not know.

Our world is filled with many people who struggle through life. They are everywhere. People living paycheck to paycheck. People struggling in dead-end jobs or failing relationships. You don't have to look far to find these people. Some only have to look in the mirror.

The sad reality is that a few will never find happiness or take advantage of a second chance in life. They will never see or seize the opportunities around them. From my days as a police officer and later as a prosecutor, I saw many failed lives. People who made the same mistakes repeatedly, who abandoned God or their higher power, who simply gave up hope or who turned to drugs, crime or alcohol as their sole salvation.

Thankfully, there are many people around us who make us smile, who motivate us to do better, who offer hope in uncertain times.

Fortunately for me, I have many successes in life. Career successes, financial freedom, travel, and a great family and friends. With all those successes, I should have no complaints. But few of us lead fairy tale lives. Misfortune happens to everyone at some point in his or her life. Disease strikes, businesses fail, relationships often hit rough spots.

Last year, my streak of good luck hit a rough patch. The firm I worked for fell on financially hard times and suddenly had to let some folks go. As the last hired, I was also the first fired. Ever the optimist, I looked at my sudden loss of work as an opportunity, a chance to start my own law firm.

Eagerly, I began ordering stationary, developing a website and scouting for new clients. What I did not anticipate were the thousands of other great lawyers that were also losing their jobs and a large number of recent law school grads that could not find any work in the field.

One very bright young lawyer I know found himself working as a part-time assistant zookeeper in charge of "cleaning up" after elephants and other large animals. Although happy to have a job, this certainly was not the career he signed up for when enrolling in law school three years earlier.

Just as these lawyers were struggling so was our new business. We happened to pick the worst economy in decades to hang out our shingle and start a business.

My earlier enthusiasm soon turned to fear. Without any money for advertising, how could we let clients know of our business and bring them to our door? How would we pay office rent? Our lack of income was beginning to weigh me down.

The legal profession was also changing. New lawyers facing tens of thousands of dollars of unpaid student loans were suddenly advertising rates so ridiculously low that we wondered if clients would even consider paying for our experience and hiring us.

Each day, the fear became worse. How much longer could I keep up with the mortgage? If suddenly finding myself unemployed at age 50 and struggling to start a new practice in the worst economy of my generation was not enough stress in my life, my beloved mother passed away.

With each passing day, the fear became worse; it turned into depression.

In November of 2010, one of my best friends called to ask for a favor. Would I accompany him to a fundraiser? I certainly was not thrilled with the idea, particularly with little money to contribute.

I attended more out of a sense of duty and did not know anything about the event other than the fact that one of our mutual friends organized it. Once there, I learned that the event was not simply a fundraiser. It was an event to celebrate the life of a young child suffering from a rare and virulent type of cancer. It was a way for the parents to give back to the community and say thanks. It was also an event to raise money for a charity that helps other families of children facing serious illness.

Not until I arrived did I learn how selfless the family was that threw this party. More importantly, not until I arrived did I realize that the little boy was the son of a mutual friend.

On my way to the event, I called my friend and pledged to stay for a few minutes of pleasantries then politely bow out. It was a Friday night after all, and I had plans to share a few cocktails with other friends at a sports bar and watch a game.

Throughout the cocktail hour, the little boy was running around the party. He ran from table to table surrounded by adults in jackets and dresses, this little boy. He was beaming, taking pictures and laughing. Surely, this could not be the boy who has cancer. He was probably the kid of some parents who couldn't find a babysitter that night.

As the dinner began, the lights were dimmed, and a media presentation began about the boy and his family. His doctors talked about the months of hospitalization, the pain, and the need for future care; his mother and father (both police officers) talked about their efforts to keep the family both solvent; and the family thanked the hundreds of caregivers, friends, and neighbors that rallied behind this little boy.

Fellow police officers and neighbors built a jungle gym in the backyard so the boy could play (he missed months of school and playgrounds). Local businesses helped grant the boy's wish to attend a Milwaukee Bucks basketball game (from the pictures, it looks like the team came through with front row seats).

This little boy who spent much of his life in the hospital and who faces a very uncertain future is the same little boy who was running around the hotel ballroom smiling and laughing.

Suddenly, my plans to "politely bow out" so I can have a beer with my friends seemed so unimportant. There would be many opportunities to go out on other nights. I had a great time that night and took home a photo of that little boy and placed it on my refrigerator.

The next morning while eating cereal, I began looking at the other pictures on my refrigerator. In particular, the one of my father, Lieutenant Howard Mahany of the U.S. Army Air Corps, proudly kneeling on the wing of his P-51 Mustang fighter plane. The plane displaying seven flags representing seven enemy aircraft destroyed.

That morning while looking at the photos on my refrigerator I learned two important lessons and returned to work on Monday with a renewed sense of energy and a much different perspective on life and work. Happily, I can say that since that morning, my fear is in check, my practice is doing very well, and again, I remember all those blessings that make me thankful for each day.

What are those two lessons learned that morning?

First, that life is precious. We need to embrace each day and the opportunities each day brings. Life is always going to throw curve balls now and then. Unfortunately, in these new economic times, people lose their jobs and homes every day. And despite many recent medical miracles, we all will die someday. The impossible odds faced by that young man suddenly put things in their proper perspective.

If we focus too much on our problems, we lose sight of the opportunities. That boy and his family could choose to focus on the pain, the bills, the lost childhood. Instead, they threw a party to thank everyone who helped them and to provide opportunities for other kids facing life-threatening illness. Don't ever try to tell that child he doesn't have the same opportunities as other kids. In some ways, he has more.

Without energy, inspiration, and motivation, life becomes more difficult. It's not enough to simply love your work. Success is inspired and sometimes that inspiration can be found in the strangest of places.

Obviously, inspiration is more than just a picture on the refrigerator. It's the realization that opportunity is everywhere if you look. I went to work on Monday that week and suddenly found all sorts of opportunities. I find my inspiration from great writers like Matt Morris, Timothy Ferriss, and their books. I find inspiration in church. And most of all, I find it through the stories of others, like the little boy on my refrigerator.

I said there were two lessons that next morning and wanted to address the other. They are equally important. The other photo on the fridge that provided me with renewed inspiration was that of my father. Dad was a fighter pilot and ace in World War II. In aerial combat, you survive by killing the enemy before he kills you. It's brutal but that simple.

Fortunately, life for most of us doesn't involve killing, but it does involve action. Anyone can spend his or her life planning, plotting and studying. The successful ones among us, however, are those that are also "doing."

Just like in combat, at some point, the planning has to stop and be replaced by action. Reading marketing books, hiring advertising consultants and developing detailed action plans have their place in any new business. No one should march into battle without a plan.

For many of us, however, we get so wrapped up in the planning that life passes us by before we take the opportunity to act.

As I said before, there are opportunities all around us. To enjoy them, however, we have to take chances and act. Our men and women in Iraq and Afghanistan take huge risks every day. Some pay the ultimate price in defense of our freedom and give their lives. The risks we take are usually not as deadly but to have any chance of success, we have to face our fears and take those risks.

What did I learn that day and the next morning? That life offers us inspiration in the most unusual places and that to succeed, we must not only be inspired but must also act decisively when opportunity knocks.

By the time this book is published, there will likely be new additions and changes to the outside of our refrigerator, but two photos will remain forever.

BIOGRAPHY

Brian Mahany is a lawyer with a national practice helping victims of fraud get back their hard-earned money. He also helps people and businesses with tax problems and those accused of white-collar crimes. A lawyer for 27 years, Brian previously served as Maine's revenue commissioner, as an assistant attorney general, and a criminal investigator. In 2008, he was part of the Wesley Snipes defense team. He lives in Milwaukee, Wisconsin.

CONTACT INFORMATION

Brian Mahany
(262) 970-8500
P.O. Box 511328, Milwaukee WI 53202
www.mahanyertl.com

CHAPTER 22

WHAT LEGACY ARE YOU GOING TO LEAVE BEHIND?

By Jill Nieman Picerno

When people think of what kind of legacy they would like to leave behind, they usually think financially. However, when I was a child, I knew that my legacy would be my children. I thought that the most important thing I could do for the world was to raise my children into becoming amazing adults. I always wanted to have two girls, sisters, as I never had a sister and always thought that would be so great. My wish did come true. I am blessed with two incredible girls. My first daughter, Jacquelyn, was born when I was 28 years old. Then two years and ten months later, Caitlyn was born. I was fortunate enough to become a Stay-At-Home Mom the day Jacquelyn was born, but this didn't just happen. My husband, at the time, and I worked very hard to pay off debts and make sure that his income would be able to provide for our family to live comfortably once I became a Stay-At-Home Mom.

I am also a CPA, and I started up my practice a little while after Jacquelyn was born. I ran my small practice from our home, which allowed me to continue being a Stay-At-Home Mom. I chose this career, while in college, specifically with this in mind. Parenting, not my CPA practice, would always be my number one job. I have read so many books about children and child raising, talked about my children and their various stages of development with my friends and family and even asked strangers their opinions about parenting. Once I began the parenting role, I set off towards creating my legacy. I knew that having an honest and completely open relationship with my girls when they were teenagers would be crucial to creating the legacy I wanted to leave behind.

Parenting is a tough job. It requires a ton of energy, and you need to realize how a parent shapes a child's future. We all want the best for our children, but sometimes, that gets lost in the day to day activities. We need to write down our goals for parenting.

Look at how you were parented. What did you like about your parents' parenting styles and what is it that you don't like about their styles?

Many of us rarely take the time to sit down and think this through. Sit down right now and take out a sheet of paper. Let your mind go back in time and remember how your parents raised you. Write down everything that comes to your mind, without stopping, letting your mind flow. Keep writing until you believe you have captured your parents' parenting styles on paper. Now the fun begins. We are all creatures of habit, so many of us just parent as we were parented. That doesn't need to be the case. What type of parenting style do you want your children to experience? How do you want your children to feel about you and them? Remember to start creating your legacy with the end in mind.

Parents often ask me how I created such an honest and completely open relationship with my girls. Many things helped create our incredible relationships along the way, but there is one rule that I have had from the beginning of my parenting role. This rule, I believe, was the foundation of my relationships with my girls. My rule from the beginning was "No Lying."

Lying is always wrong. My girls learned at a very early age to speak the truth which was not a very easy task to accomplish. Children will lie to their parents. They lie to their parents to avoid being punished for something they did wrong in their parent's eyes. My girls did not like to be punished, like all children, but they did lie to me to avoid being punished. They soon figured out though that when they lied to me to avoid being punished, their punishment became ten times worse than if they had just told me the truth from the beginning.

They also learned that if they did tell me the truth right away about what they had done wrong, they wouldn't get in as much trouble as if I had caught them in the act. This was a little bit of a reward for telling the truth right away. Both my girls learned this rule and realized that telling the truth had its benefits.

Honesty is something their mother values. If my girls were not honest with me and lied, I would be very disappointed in them. Children do not want to disappoint their parents. Children just want to avoid getting punished. Parents should try to catch their children lying at an early age and instill in them the value of honesty.

Become a great detective. Learn the body signals that occur when someone is lying to you. Children will usually delay answering your initial questions. When they finally do answer your questions, their voice will have a slightly higher pitch to it. Their hands may cover their mouth or rub their nose often. Facial expressions will change. Their face may look paler and stiffer, their nostrils may flare, and their lips may look thinner and tighter. Avoiding direct eye contact, squinting or closing their eyes may also give them away. Their body may become stiffer, shoulders may be pulled up, and their elbows may be held close to their body. These are just a few of the body signals that parents may want to be on the lookout for.

Once you do know your child is lying, take action. Do not explain to them how you know they are lying. All they need to know is that you know they lied. Then tell them this is unacceptable. Explain to them the first punishment they were going to receive for having the inappropriate behavior. Then let them know that since they lied to you about what did happen, the punishment will be ten times the initial punishment they would have received.

Remember to have the punishment fit the inappropriate behavior, but make sure it is something you can and will follow through with. Your child also needs to realize that you were upset about their inappropriate behavior, but you are so much more disappointed in the fact that they felt the need to lie to you. Children lie to avoid punishment, but they do not want to disappoint you and lying creates disappointment.

When children start to reach the teenage years, this lying rule needs to be set in stone. You still need to be able to detect the body signals your child exposes to you when he/she is lying.

We must also realize that this age is a very difficult stage in your child's development. Try to remember how you felt or acted like as a teenager. Yes, that does scare some of us, and we don't want our children to make some of the same mistakes we did.

They do need to make some of their own mistakes, as they don't always learn from being told what to do and what not do. Being overly strict parents is not the course of action that seems to produce the best results related to some of their teenager's actions. I do believe this, as I know things about my female friends that their parents would not believe about their teenagers if I told them. Parents need to not parent with blinders on. The information I know about their friends becomes handy when trying to steer them towards a better path in life.

Teenagers are influenced by their friends more than their parents. You have to be one of their friends too. Always be the parent first and their friend second. Teenagers will not tell you that they like you being their parent and setting rules, but this honestly does make them feel loved. They know you care about what happens to them.

My girls think some of my rules are a little over the top, but they understand my reasoning behind my rules. They know they are loved. It's a fine line between having too many rules or too few rules or too strict rules or not strict enough rules. Hopefully, with this point, you have built that honest and completely open relationship with your children, as this will help guide you in setting your own rules for your teenagers.

This brings me to a question that has come up with my girls. Should I treat my girls the same related to the rules I have; yes and no. Yes, some rules should be the same, but every teenager is different. I remember having dinner with my girls one night, and Caitlyn began talking about one of her friends drinking her parent's alcohol. I asked Caitlyn, "Which friend is that?" Caitlyn proceeded to tell me, in so many words, that it was none of my business and she didn't want me to tell her parents. I then explained to her that she did not need to tell me which friend of hers was doing this, but then she would suffer the consequences of my parenting rules being differently related to her than her sister.

Of course, life is not fair. I continued explaining to Caitlyn that Jacquelyn has told me many things about her friends and I haven't mentioned it to her friend's parents. My trust with Jacquelyn will be higher, and she will have more privileges related to hanging out with her friends than Caitlyn would. Needless to say, Caitlyn decided to tell me which friend of hers was drinking her parent's alcohol and we moved on from there. I have always kept my girl's secrets about their friends safe with me, except for one time. The only time I believe that I should tell another parent something about their teenager that my girls have shared with me in confidence is if it can be life-threatening. I got my daughter's permission to talk to the teenager's parents, as she was worried about her friend's life as well. Everything, fortunately, turned out great.

The teenage years are always interesting. I love that my girls feel so comfortable coming to me with any questions that they may have, but when the teenage years rolled around, their questions became life path altering.

Their questions became more about sex, drugs, boys, girls and so many other important topics about life in general.

Sometimes when one of my girls would come to ask me a question, inside, I am freaking out, but on the outside, I act as they asked me "What are we doing for dinner?" I was so proud of my girls being able to ask me any question they felt they wanted an answer about.

My girls realize that I don't know everything, but I told them we could always find out the answer together.

One question I remember one of my girls asking me was "Will you die if you have sex before you are 19 years old?" My daughter was just entering her teenage years, and one of her friend's moms had told her friend that. So began the talk about sex. I did tell her that "You do not die if you have sex before you are 19 years old." I think that the mother was trying to protect her daughter but didn't have an open relationship with her daughter to talk things out. This then led us into a conversation about AIDs, STDs, etc. The questions my girls came to ask were always a time to have discussions, and for me to steer them in the right direction. I realized that no one person can control another person. So I have tried to give my girls as much information as I thought necessary for them to make the correct choices in life. My girls and I are so glad we have this honest and completely open relationship. It hasn't always been easy, but it's always been worth it.

My life path continues today on creating a legacy for my incredible girls. This is how I measure success.

Biography

Jill Nieman Picerno is a very proud mother and entrepreneur. She is a student of parenting, finance, real estate and network marketing. She has thrust for knowledge, loves to meet new people, and visit new places around the world. She is a Certified Public Accountant, owns several real estate properties and has her own travel business, www.travelgirls.biz. She is also in the process of creating her very own parenting book.

CONTACT INFORMATION

Jill Nieman Picerno
10940 S Parker Rd, Ste 472
Parker,CO 80134
303-400-5100
jill@travelgirls.biz

Chapter 23

MY SUCCESS IS ACHIEVED BY CREATING STRONG RELATIONSHIPS

By Andre' Serraile

My parents were both born in Louisiana in the 1930s; this was a time when people had to be strong to survive. My father's mother, my grandmother, was a maid and she made about $40 a month and his father, my grandfather, was a chef. Sadly, things didn't work out, and my grandparents split up. My grandfather moved to New Orleans. He died before I was born. Now my father was being raised by a single parent. Back then there was no welfare, as I understood at that point in history. If a person couldn't find work back then, well, you can guess the alternatives. Living during the Great Depression was tough.

My mother was the oldest of a large family of 14. My grandfather on my mother's side died early too. My grandmother remarried and had two more children; this is the reason for the large family. Now, my father had help being raised by my great uncle, who had started an insurance company in the small town where he lived. My father was thus learning about business from an early age. My great uncle, my grandmother's brother, showed him how to be a man. His son, my father's cousin, became like a brother to him and my father made him my godfather. My father would run a paper route, giving him even more early experience in business. However, that was not enough to help his mother out, so, he quit high school to join the Navy. He served in the Korean War, 1950-1955, working in the searing heat of the boiler room. He sent money home to my grandmother and even paid off the mortgage on the house.

Nevertheless, my father eventually came back home and met my mother. They were married. Sadly, soon after my grandfather passed on.

Therefore, even before I was born, both my actual grandfathers on both sides had died, along with my grandmother on my father's side. As a result, my mother's step-father was the only grandfather I knew, and I had only one grandmother alive, who was on my mother's side. It didn't matter though; he set a great example as a carpenter that worked very hard. He also was in the Army. I believe he served in WWII. I was brought up to believe that no matter what, blood begets blood and family was family. For example, even though my mother had step-brothers, they were her brothers. And I was taught that my mother's step-brothers were my uncles. No exceptions.

Now, my parents moved to Tyler, Texas. My mother was considering becoming a nurse. My father tried to secure work, but he soon attempted to reenlist in the Navy, but they said they don't take men with dependents. So, he walked out that office and into the Air Force office, rejoining the service as an airman. He went to serve in West Germany, before its reunification. He sent for my mother and my brother and I were born there. Now, I was too young to remember anything, so I didn't learn any German. Soon, however, we came back to the US, and while riding in a car back to Louisiana, I had my first birthday. So I guess that is why I love traveling so much. Later, when we were living in California, my sister was born. Fortunately, my parents had a game plan to give us all a better life. My mother wanted to go to college. The plan was set in motion after my father took a tour of duty in Vietnam from 1964-1967. He was an aircraft mechanic that serviced F111 fighter-bombers after flight missions. My mother started college at Grambling State University during this period. My brother, sister, and I stayed at my grandparents. My father would send money to pay for college and some to my grandmother to keep me and my siblings fed.

I was about two years old when my father left, so I couldn't remember what he looked like. When he came home from Vietnam, I was five, and my mother had to reintroduce me to my father, saying, "André, this your Daddy." I just told myself, okay then, this is my father. Now, I say all this to show that a goal can be achieved if you don't make excuses; my parents are a great example, and young children are flexible because they don't know any better. My mother and father made their sacrifices to create a better lifestyle for their family. So, that event shaped my thinking that sacrifices are usually made to achieve a greater goal.

Next, my father received orders for Nellis Air Force Base in Las Vegas, Nevada. At that time, the population of Las Vegas was only 64,405. My mother graduated from college and became a teacher. She secured a contract the Clark County School District and started teaching at a high school. My parents liked Las Vegas, so they said, "This is home." Well, when I started to attend school, my father took me fishing on the weekends. On Sundays, my parents took us to church. He brought me up to love listening to music and watching sports at this early age. By the time I was in the fourth grade, I had been given a violin, and I was taking lessons at school. Well, integration was introduced, so I took a bus to another school. I told my new band director that I was learning violin and he said: "I don't teach violin." I told my father, and he said, "Try out this cornet," and I told my new band director I was going to learn this instrument instead. He said, "Good. I can teach you how to play it."

At this time, I was exploring the desert lots around the town, and I would collect nuts and bolts and other things and put them into jars because I believed they could be useful for something. I had also been a cub scout. Then I heard that people were saying that I would be a businessman because I saw an opportunity in everything. I started playing flag football. The team won second place in the league. When I started junior high school, I tried out for the basketball team and the track team and got cut. I had an interest in tennis, and I was asked to play on the golf team. Well, I shot a 103! However, I was improving on my cornet, and I was excited about my progress. So, this became my real focus. Soon, I was playing and marching in parades.

When I got to high school as a freshman, I played in the marching and concert bands. I joined a band that played for a special choir group the choir director had formed. We performed various styles of music including pop, country, rock, and soul. As a sophomore, I became the lead trumpet player for all the bands. I even made superior marks for city solo ensemble and attended Nevada State solo ensemble. I had also got selected for Clark County Honor Bands and was selected to perform in the Nevada State Honor Band.

My mentor was Mr. Tom Porrello. He was a phenomenal lead trumpet player and played across the country. He played for many entertainers, like jazz drummer icon, Buddy Rich, and the celebrated singer, Frank Sinatra. He gave me some good advice. He suggested not to major in music. Learn something different in college, so, you can get work and not just be a struggling musician.

It's feast or famine in that business. If I had developed my talent, I could go back and attend music school later. Well, that's what he suggested, but I learned music on my own from real musicians in Las Vegas. Now, earlier I had an interest in becoming a lawyer or a pilot, or maybe both. But I guess music was my main concern back then. As mentioned, during this time and even while in junior high school, I had developed an interest in business. I had also learned how to type, and I would type term papers and thesis for students and doctoral candidates at Northern Arizona University, where my mother was getting her master's. I would charge 25 cents a page. I made $125 one summer.

I participated actively in high school and had been involved in many organizations, like the National Honor Society, the Senior and Junior Cabinets, and Boy State. College came into the picture, but I was undecided about which one to attend. Well, my mother suggested I also go to Grambling State University and that the band department was good too. My father told me, starting from when I was about 15, that I should be ready to make a decision about what direction to take because at 18 years of age, I would not be living in his house. I would joke around about it, but I knew he was serious. If not college, it would be the military or, if I found a job, he would let me stay for a few months more to save up money for an apartment. Frankly, I was more than ready to leave for college because I was ready to get some background knowledge to start a business. One week after my high school graduation, that summer after, I left for Grambling State University, and I thought it would be nice to learn the campus layout and get a head start taking some courses. So this way I would be able to hit the ground running for the Fall Semester.

Also, during the summer I could attend band camp. I had received a band scholarship. I applied for other scholarships too. These scholarships covered my first two years of my college education. I had also received an Army ROTC scholarship. The Army paid for the last two years of my college education with books included. I had learned a lesson in the process of getting the Army scholarship. I really wanted the pilot scholarship for Air Force ROTC, but the officer in charge told me that it would be a slim chance of getting it. So, I went complaining to the Army when I should have waited to see my financial statement. I came back for the fall and found out that I did receive the pilot scholarship. I was very upset. I had learned a big lesson to be patient and never let anyone put doubts in my mind.

I had two educators that influenced me in leadership skills. One was the band director for the famous GSU Tiger Marching Band, Prof. Conrad Hutchinson Jr. and the head football coach, the legendary Eddie Robinson of the Grambling State University Football Team. Prof. Hutchinson Jr. was a strict disciplinarian in regard to musical performing and following the schedule. He did not like you being late for anything. I had the opportunity to travel to perform at Yankee Stadium in New York City and Tokyo, Japan. Also, I appeared in the famous Coca-Cola commercial.

Unmistakably, meeting Coach Eddie Robinson was an honor and a privilege. Yet the coach was a very humble man, albeit driven for excellence in his coaching role for the GSU Football Team. His greatest accomplishment was to be named, "The Most Winningest Coach in College Football" with 408 wins. All his wins were at Grambling State University. He taught me a lot about leadership skills by example. By the way, his wife, Doris, his son Eddie Jr., daughter, Rose, and his grandchildren had accepted myself and my sister, who also graduated from GSU, as family. I used to visit Coach Eddie at his home regularly.

Ultimately, I was commissioned as a US army officer in the Armor Division. I left for Fort Knox, Kentucky for basic officer training. I had not received my diploma yet. I had to take the necessary courses and sent the credit hours back to Grambling, and they sent my diploma to me while I was training. Through this, I have learned it does matter how you achieve your goal, as long as you accomplish it. After training, I was informed that it was my choice not to accept activity duty, so I decided to enter the civilian world because I wanted to get some work experience that I could someday use in my entrepreneurial endeavors.

To this end, I moved to Los Angeles, California for a job in a silicone factory. I was working in the quality control department. Well, because of an event that occurred at this job, I left to consider other options. However, I didn't quit. It was a leave of absence. During that period, my mother called me and said my father was sick and he requested that I come home to help her. So, I had a meeting with my boss, and he said I could come back, but I told him thanks, but I need to be at home to help my father. I felt that commuting back and forth from Las Vegas, Nevada to help my father would be taxing on me mentally.

Nevertheless, it proved to be a spiritual experience with my father. One day, we had a discussion about Jesus. He told me that without Jesus, you could not enter heaven and I that should continue to attend church. I had always attended as often as I could, but I had made a commitment to make it an important activity in my life. As he always told me, your word is your bond and if you say you are going to commit, follow through. If you can't, tell them that you can't commit, call that person and cancel. I felt so blessed to have a father like mine. He taught me the value of honest work, and he took me fishing, and that taught me about patience. He also told me that he and my mother had achieved a lot, yet he told me not to wait for the inheritance. He challenged me to strive for greater success. During that time, I had worked as a management trainee at a rental car agency for about a year, but it didn't work out. The next year, I worked as a supervisor for the detention center, downtown. I had also attended a casino dealer school and passed, yet I didn't look for work at the casinos. Unfortunately, things didn't work out at the detention center, so I started and completed the process of becoming a substitute teacher. Well, it was that time, during the summer, in July, my father passed away.

As I moved on from the death of my father, that fall, I started work as a substitute teacher. I stayed busy because I was not picky about what grade or subject area I taught. Consequently, during my first high school reunion, I met a fellow band member and told him that I was a substitute teacher. He said that he was a casino dealer. I had mentioned that I had attended dealer school but never started dealing. He admonished me that I could be good at it and I should start working as a casino dealer. Therefore, I started work as a craps dealer and, after I was able to, I also took substitute teaching assignments too. I had considered going back and getting my student teacher credentials and teaching full time. I had been accepted onto a program at Louisiana Tech University in Ruston, LA. I decided to decline because I believed that I would gain some fantastic people skills working in the casino. Years later, I had thought that, if I can get an IT degree, I can get into computer programming and eventually start a computer consulting business. However, after a while, I realized that I was not that committed to such a role. If I had started looking for an IT job the moment I had graduated, I might have transitioned into that field. However, I waited two years to start looking. I was too confident that I could find an IT position. I had received temporary work with shipping software for UPS, but I stopped the training because the hours were hard to keep because of my current job. So, I did have a path to IT, but, for whatever reason, I had reservations about my career direction.

As a result, I had learned from that event, and I had to reconsider my career path. Moreover, I had transferred to a role in a new hotel and casino. After a few years working there, I wanted to look for an opportunity where I could provide a service where there were no limitations, and which created a cash flow. I had looked into the real estate investment business, but I found out that I had to know what I was doing. It may not be important to some, but I knew you could get into trouble quickly if you don't know about the laws concerning real estate. To my surprise, I consulted a realtor about the laws, and I was advised to attend real estate school. I had researched and found out that if I put in the work, I can do well as a realtor and I can become an investor too. Also, I had read that it doesn't take a large capital outlay and brokerages provided office space and other resources and training.

Now, I had set a year to start a real estate school. After this, I had looked at a photo of myself taken at a Super Bowl party. I had noticed that I was overweight. I worked out, but, after research, I had found that going into my 50s, I couldn't eat like I did when I was in my 20s or 30s. I found a new diet and workout, and I went from 183 pounds to 154 pounds. I was so excited that I enjoyed telling others about my weight loss. Now, after my weight loss success, I was even more enthusiastic to start real estate school.

I had visited a couple of brokerages before I started. So I had decided to become a realtor. Therefore, I attended a real estate course online, and I took the real estate exam and failed. I found some resources and studied harder, and I then passed. Later, I was offered the opportunity to become a realtor at Berkshire Hathaway HomeServices Nevada Properties.

In conclusion, I am actively and continually striving to achieve as an entrepreneur. So, I would not say I am just a realtor, but also someone aspiring to provide value to others. I have elevated my sights above the status quo of what most accept. Desire, determination, discipline, and decisiveness are what I strive to maintain. I have learned that I live in a country where anyone can succeed, contrary to what some may say, that living in the United States has limitations. Here is a conversation I had with a military officer from Lebanon. He told me never to take my country for granted. He said that he could not believe that he sees people on the streets of the United States begging for money. He explained that the country he is from uses a caste system. If you were born to a family where your father is a medical doctor, you too could be a doctor. If you were born to a father who was a laborer, you are assigned a position as a laborer. You are not allowed to become a doctor. So, I beg to differ, if anyone here in the US has no chance to become successful. I challenge you to take advantage of the opportunities that are available to learn and develop your abilities and create your wealth, be it monetary, in relationships, or spiritually.

Biography

What makes Andre' Serraile an authority is that he has learned that his success is achieved by creating strong relationships and not striving to create an abundance of wealth. As he applies this principle to build and strengthen his relationships with his clients, he continues to study his craft and invest in improving himself.

Contact Information

Facebook: https://www.facebook.com/andre.serraile
LinkedIn: https://www.linkedin.com/in/andre-serraile-8b25141b/
YouTube: https://www.youtube.com/channel/UCTJkzCXJdB0TeGSJ_I1I5xg
Twitter: https://twitter.com/JazzyDre
Instagram: https://www.instagram.com/andresixpackabs.com_/
Website: https://www.andreserraile.com
Blog: https://andreserraile.wordpress.com/

Chapter 24
THE DANCE LIFE

By Blake Elder

My name is Blake Elder. I was born in Cleburne, Texas, in 1963. I was raised in a family of four by my parents, Bobby and Joyce, and my brother, Wade. We lived on a 110-acre farm just Southeast of Cleburne, Texas, in a little community called San Flats. Growing up, my Dad was always ambitious as he was able to thrive as a superintendent, school teacher, and a coach. With my dad working full time, my mom stayed home with us until I started 1st grade.

My family was very active in the sport of rodeo. My parents competed in many arenas performing various events including Bareback and Bull Riding, Steer Wrestling and Barrel Racing. My Mother even rode Bulls. They were so involved that they also announced, judged, and kept time for competitions. Following my parents lead, my brother and I participated in rodeo as we grew older.

Throughout my childhood, my family moved a couple of times. When I was five years old, my family moved to Blum, Texas, which is where I obtained my grade school education. Later, when I was 10, we moved to a place just west of Weatherford, Texas, called Brock. We stayed in Brock through the rest of my education and my family still lives there today.

I was a member of several clubs, including Future Farmers of America, Beta, Varsity Basketball, and the Rodeo team. After high school, I attended Weatherford Junior college for two years to get my foundation classes out of the way. At the time, I wasn't sure what I wanted to major in; I knew I wanted to do something to help people or in the teaching field, but I also wanted to make money and not struggle. I knew teachers did not have a high income, but with my basics out of the way, unbeknownst to me at the time, I was laying the groundwork and practicing for my future career by going out and dancing.

After graduating with my Associates Degree from Weatherford Jr. college, I transferred to Tarleton State University in Stephenville, Texas. At university, I was able to help start a fraternity, Delta Chi, and work at a local photo shop. In 1987, I graduated from Tarleton with a Bachelor of Science in Physical Education. This degree has allowed me to teach and coach basketball.

Throughout college, I held numerous jobs. My college career began with owning a photography business, where I took wedding portraits, graduation pictures, and Christmas photos. Two of my unique work experiences came later as I got a job at the Campus Corner doing party pictures for all the clubs, Sororities, and Fraternities on campus. It's not often that you get paid to attend campus parties. My second favorite was working at the local movie theatre as a projectionist. That job came with the perk of free movies.

While attending Tarleton, I danced in and won several dance competitions. I had a lot of fun and great partners who helped expand my love for dance. These college dance experiences helped me learn a lot about people and dance.

After graduation, I moved to Fort Worth, Texas, and got a job at a local dance studio. A year of working there, I realized I didn't enjoy working for someone else. I talked to the owners of a local C&W nightclub about renting space to teach lessons.

The owners of the C&W club agreed to let me rent space which led to me opening my own dance studio; therefore, in 1987 I opened my dance studio named "The Blake Elder Dance Center." Opening my own studio allowed me to take my work from part-time to full-time. While building my name and clientele, I juggled working at my dance studio and various clubs such as at West Side Stories, Cheyenne Cattle Company, and the Horseman club.

During that time, I got a call from a friend who taught at The University of Texas at Arlington. I got a job teaching there in 1995 and taught for 15 years. I taught 10 to 12 dance classes with 150 students and coached 4 to 6 basketball classes with 50 to 80 students each week every semester, which was a lot of work for little pay, but I loved it. For any of the students who wanted to learn more than the basic patterns I taught at the University, they would come to my studio for privates or group classes, which was a great marketing tool for my dance business.

In 2010, the Affordable Care Act became law, and it resulted in laying off several part-time teachers from the University, including me. The law put new restrictions on the University, which led to budget cuts. Unfortunately, I only got a 4-day notice.

This lay off led me to get serious about my studio, dance business, and network marketing. I was involved with a network marketing business called Stream Energy as well as several home-based startups. No matter how successful, I learned something from all of them.

I found out in the dance world that I had to focus on budgeting and planning. There are three months out of the year that business drops and revenue decreases. Due to low revenue during those three months, I knew I had to do something besides dance during those times. That's why network marketing looked so attractive to me; I didn't want to have a second job. I wanted to build something in which I was able to do the work once but got paid repeatedly.

Dance Life is the title I chose for my chapter because I have been dancing, competing, and teaching for over 35 years. Therefore, I lived and breathed dance for more than three decades.

With that being said, I've been self-employed for 30 years. I've been blessed to have taught group classes in over 20 Clubs including Cowboys Arlington, and now at Cowboys Red River in Dallas, Texas, I taught 15 years at the University of Texas in Arlington and helped put together and write the rules for the World's Richest Amateur Dance Competition. My friend called me and said Marlboro & Country Club Dance Enterprises wants to run a national dance competition. My friend was the national event coordinator, and he asked me to put together the rules, for the dances, and judges. I agreed, and we hosted dance contests in over 70 clubs the first year, and over 100 clubs the next three years. The National Finals were held at Cowboys in Arlington, Texas and Marlboro paid up to $10,000 for the 1st place in that dance competition.

Being in the dance scene has given me great opportunities to achieve success and help my students achieve success. My Dance Partners and I won 15 to 20 local club competitions in the late '80s, '90s and early 2000s, I have competed on the Country and Western and Swing Circuit for 15+ years. I've placed in many Jack & Jill contests and took 2nd in the showcase. Many of the students I taught ended up taking top honors, and some went on to teach professionally. This was all fun but a lot of hard work to consistently travel; therefore, it was time to stay local and not travel to compete. Instead, I focused on teaching others the joy of dancing and coaching others who want to compete.

I made a significant adjustment in life when I decided to change what I did. I stopped competing and focused on teaching at more clubs and coaching others at my studio.

Through this change in life, it opened so many opportunities for me to grow professionally and personally. I have taught well over 50,000 people to dance and have judged hundreds of dance competitions. I was the event coordinator for the World's Richest Amateur Dance Competition at the time, The Marlboro Country Dance Showdown. For four years, I ran a weekly Jack & Jill contest every Tuesday night at the Cheyenne Cattle Company. I was asked to manage several clubs throughout my career but declined the offer due to wanting to stick to the entertainment side of the business – not the bar side.

Bringing me back to my rodeo days growing up, I have been a member for 17 years and on the Board of Directors for the RCA Rodeo Cowboys Alumni. This association gives college scholarships to kids that perform rodeo in high school and make it to nationals. We do two big fundraising events each spring at Billy Bob's Texas or nearby restaurants. Each winter during the National Finals Rodeo (NFR) we hold an event at the Orleans Hotel and Casino in Las Vegas. In 2019, I was honored to be elected President of the RCA, Rodeo Cowboy Alumni.

Despite being busy and involved in the community, I help take care of my active elderly mother who still lives alone in her home. She requires a helping hand 2 to 3 days a week to do household chores. I've had to learn how to manage time efficiently to keep her prioritized. That being said, it is good to keep in mind the definition of insanity. That insanity is "doing the same thing over and over again and expecting a different result." I found out in life that practice does not make perfect, rather we need to ensure we are performing correct repetition to achieve the desired result.

Dance Life 5
Myth: Practice Makes Perfect

Truth: Correct Repetition Makes Perfect
Repetition reinforces good habits while striving for perfection.
Perfect *Practice Makes Perfect!*
Correct *Repetition Makes Perfect!*
If you do not perform a habit correctly, then you reinforce that bad habit repeatedly. This applies to all facets of life: personal relationships, business relationships, coworkers, and subordinates.

Throughout many years of experience, I have had the opportunity to run a dance studio, teach at clubs, teach at the University, and manage several network marketing companies. During this array of experiences, one idea seems to always hold true about finding clients, customers, or business partners:
Those Who Do, Will
Those Who Don't, Won't
If a person wants something badly enough, then they do what needs to happen to achieve that goal or complete that task. Often, if someone wants something to happen but do not have the means, then they will call in reinforcements by hiring an employee or asking a friend for help. When someone asks a friend to be part of a business with them, there are many pitfalls to be cautious of. First, the friend may not be very helpful at the business due to lack of knowledge or interest in the business. Another pitfall to be cautious of is adequate training. If you hire a friend as an employee, it is imperative to adequately train them and encourage them in the work they are doing. This will help motivate the person and help the person feel they make a difference at the company.

When you bring someone into your business, you will need to take the employee by the hand and show them the processes of the business. This will help the new employee know their duties and responsibilities while gaining small successes. By helping the employee succeed, the employee's confidence increases.

If you get hired for a position at a traditional job, then the company that hired you will put you through training so that you can perform your job duties well. Sales, or network marketing, functions in the same way. Although you're in business for yourself, you are not doing business alone. Throughout the process, you will run into hearing the word "no." Being successful means looking for the "no" to get to the next "YES." To be able to do this, you must separate yourself emotionally from the "no." Do not take the "no" personally but see it as your next step to get to a "yes."

If I stopped dancing because someone said no when I asked or stopped teaching when a student didn't buy a private lesson, then I would not be in business today.

If you don't ask, you will never get what you want.
Therefore, keep getting told "no" until you find a "YES!"

Dance Life 6
Helping People

No Earning Without Learning

To get where you want to go in life and business, you need to surround yourself with people who have qualities you want in yourself. You should surround yourself with people who are hungry for knowledge and growth. For example, if you desire to be a well-managed business owner, then surround yourself with successful business owners who manage their time well.

Successful people will say, "I would rather have 1% of 100 people's efforts than 100% of my own efforts." This saying rings true because if the person giving 100% can't work, then the business doesn't make money. Although, if I have 100 people giving 1 percent of themselves, then the business will still be able to run.

In network marketing, I can get the one percent from people, instead of requiring 100% from myself. This allows the business to go beyond me and run on its own. That's what initially attracted me to network marketing: you do the work once but get paid out repeatedly. Therefore, if you build enough business, network marketing can be sustainable and profitable.

In the dance world, I had two choices when clients master the skill I taught them: look for a new client or teach the current client the value in continuing lessons. If I look for a new client once the client learns a set of patterns or moves, then replacing that client would cost me my time and money. Instead, I would rather remind the student of the value in lessons and explain new patterns and techniques they can learn if they continue lessons.

As long as you keep these three things in mind, success should come:

- Helping them learn. Help your employees learn the responsibilities and duties of their new role, so they do not feel overwhelmed.
- Helping them solve a problem. Some examples are learning new moves, time management, or how to save money.
- Care about the people. Caring about people will allow your employees to be loyal to you and your company.

The Dance Life 7
Recruiting Steps

A. Recruiting
1. You want to look for **quality** not **quantity** when it comes to business partners or associates for your team. Quantity will come as your team grows.
2. Work smarter not harder. Ensure you are working strategically so that you do not work hard unnecessarily.
3. It is easier to work with willing, like-minded, enthusiastic people, rather than try to push, sway, manipulate or sell someone on a business or service. Even if the client may **need** the service, if they do not see the value or have a desire, then it is not worth the energy convincing them.
4. Work with the living, not the dead. If you are working with someone who is unmotivated, then find a new person and watch your business take off.
5. Stop trying to resurrect the dead; if someone on your team is not working on the business or is pulling you down, then let them go and find a new person.
6. You are just one new person away from being a big success. Keep pushing yourself to find that next person to take your business to the next step.

B. NaySayers

1. Be aware of those trying to thwart your dreams, goals, and business. These people want you to fail; therefore, you should be cautious around them or avoid them if possible.
2. If you have friends that are negative towards your business and they are not open-minded to be a positive supporter, then change your friends. You need a healthy support system.
3. If you help enough people get what they want in business or life, then you will likely get what you want out of business and life.
4. Pay yourself first, no matter how much you make. Take 10 to 20% off the top for savings, 10% for taxes, 10% for an emergency fund, then live off the rest. By doing this, you will pay the necessities while saving. By living below your means, you'll hopefully never get into a financial struggle. Then when your business takes off, you can adjust those percentages accordingly.
5. Tying into the previous point, spend less than you make. Don't buy unnecessary items you don't need. Live below your means so that you can invest in your business.

The Dance Life 8

(B I I Y) Believe and Invest in Yourself
1. **(B I Y)** Believe in yourself
2. (**I I Y**) Invest In yourself
   You have to Believe in what you're doing in order to invest in the Process.
3. You have to **Believe** to **Achieve.**
4. If you think you can or you think you can't, then you're right!
5. Read a motivational book daily, even if it's only a few pages. Or, listen to inspirational CD's or audiobooks while driving to and from work or appointments. You will be surprised at the results of your improved attitude and inspiration.
6. Below is the: Leg Weights Method System by **Blake Elder Dance.**
   Sometimes people have trouble learning certain patterns,

moves, combinations, frame, connection, etc. As a teacher, after showing them a set of patterns or a certain pattern combination several times, I will switch gears and start to show them a different, more advanced pattern or a combination. When that occurs, the student usually doesn't pick up the new move, but that's expected. I don't expect the student to have perfected the move, but after trying the new and very difficult pattern several times, I will switch back to the much easier pattern they were having trouble with before. Now, the original pattern that was once difficult seems easy and familiar because they begin to remember the pattern and feel more successful than when they tried the harder set of moves. It's like wearing leg weights while running or working out; when you take them off, you feel lighter and more energized. This way of teaching can be a great way to help students learn.
7. You must push students to learn. Begin to challenge them and review material to check for understanding. If a goal or task is completed and the student understands, then continue to progress. If not, repeat the difficult task until the student finds success.
8. Always be kind and encouraging with your team, associates, students, and recruits. Do not only instruct by word but lead by example; show them a step by step path to success, and you will find success as well.

The Dance Life 9
Quotes I Like by Blake Elder

1. You will never dance if you don't ask someone to join you, or say "yes" when someone asks you to. Start saying "yes" and taking chances.
2. If you must take action, then you must take it with proper coaching and guidance.
3. Moments of clarity or inspiration with opportunity are few and far between. Therefore, being able to recognize them as an opportunity and act on them can make you a winner. In the end, some money and success may come, or you'll be able to help others achieve their goals and dreams.

4. Remember, only you can change you. If You Choose To.
5. In Dancing, People always come up and ask me after they see me dancing at a high level with one of my Dance Partners and say: WOW! That looks great! I want to Dance Like that. How fast can I learn that? Thinking they can come in and do a few lessons and be great or competing in a month or less, what they fail to realize is how many hours of Practice time it takes to learn the moves or patterns in a specific Dance to certain types of Music, and how many thousands of hours of floor time out Dancing and Perfecting your craft, plus rehearsal time to always try to improve whatever style of Dance you are working on.

They see the Finished Product of Smooth Moves and Musicality, the SHOW, not the Blood, Sweat, and Tears; the CORRECT REPETITION it took to get there and make it look easy, effortless and as close to "PERFECT" as you can. Anyone can learn to Dance if they are willing to put in the time.

Closing

Thank you for reading my chapter, I've devoted my Life and Career to teaching and helping others to achieve their Goals and Dreams, whether in Business or to learn the Beautiful Art and Joy of Dancing. I've stayed committed to my Passion of Dancing, Competing and Teaching Dance through Good and Bad Times and wanted to share these experiences that have truly made me successful, to help and inspire others.

BIOGRAPHY

Blake Elder is driven and defined by his Faith in God. A Higher Power is always at work within him to do better. His happiness comes from helping people, whether it is a student learning to dance, a young couple perfecting their wedding dance, or the success of a business partner.

Contact Information

Facebook: https://www.facebook.com/BlakeElderDance/
LinkedIn: https://www.linkedin.com/in/blake-elder-b2b66122/
Website: http://blakeelderdance.com/

Chapter 25

RESCUED INTO MANHOOD

By Frank Mbanusi

One decade ago, I sat in a jail cell. Looking up at the rusty underside of the top bunk, I could only focus on the fear. I was filled with so much anger towards myself. I was no longer worthy of belonging. "How in the world did I get here?" The success I claimed fatally crashed back down to earth under that cell ceiling. I was now a nobody with my future hopes gone. The worst part? I had done what I had vowed never to do, become like my father. I walked in his very footsteps; creating the same results.

I am opening up about my story with a new hope that sharing a part of me will speak to any man out there who thinks, "I'm the only one with my problem," or "there's no hope for me," or "I have failed as a man, a father or a husband." Whatever your situation, you're not the only one. How I got to jail, that doesn't matter. But what I learned after hitting rock bottom, makes me the man I am today.

My Story

I am the oldest son in a single-parent family of five kids. Let that sink in. Five kids. One mom. If you asked her today, she'd tell you, "I couldn't have done it without my Heavenly Father." My mom gifted me with a profoundly spiritual, Christian faith shaping my path to purpose.

I have only scattered memories of my father. On one end of the spectrum, I remember the surprise McDonald's kids' meals he'd pick up for me on his way home from work. On the other, I remember angry yelling and pictures shattering. I would cower and cry. Somehow, those broken family pictures would always make their way back up on the walls, taped up and in new frames purchased by my mother. The very last time I saw my father I watched him be dragged away by officers. That 7-year-old vowed, "I will not be that man."

From that age, my experience of negative masculinity haunted me. I grew up angry at my father for the things I experienced and blamed him for his absence in my life. Every day, led by my mother, we would pray for him; praying he would change his ways and come back home to be the father we needed. Needless to say, there were other plans God had for our family; great plans, even through tragedy.

As best I can tell, my middle-school years were pretty much the typical middle schooler's experience. I didn't really have an identity. I wasn't popular, and kids made fun of me at times. I tried to fit in where I could, choosing to be unnoticed above excluded. And yet, rejection reared its ugly head over and over. At the age of 12, I didn't have the skills to manage pain, and the world of pornography easily sucked me in; addiction proved to be a stronghold for many more years to come causing a ripple effect into many other parts of my life.

Surviving middle school, I found status in high school sports; most notably track & field. Bent over, with my feet pushed hard back into the blocks was the only place I felt like I meant something. I was good, and everybody knew it. I loved being recognized for my accomplishments in the ink of school announcements and newspaper publications. I desperately performed for that love and attention.

I carried the same desperation into relationships. Without a foundation or guidance, I went in and out of unhealthy hookups. I felt the need to please everyone else just to get a dose of being wanted and liked. My self-worth was dirt-low. Without a father in my life, the best blueprint to manhood came from TV shows like Family Matters, Full House, and MTV. I did not realize at the time how much that had molded my thoughts, feelings, and actions for the next phase of my life.

False Start

When 9/11 rocked the world, I found my next purpose. Being from Jersey, the destruction of the Twin Towers hit way too close to home. I enlisted in the United States Marine Corps. Talk about growing up fast. At the age of 19, this was exactly what I needed. I thought.

Fast forward a few years. After a successful enlistment full of accolades and recognition from family and friends, it led to a rare opportunity to jump into the corporate world to start a dream career. I felt like I had it all. At least so I thought. By the age of 25, I was at the top of the achievement table by most standards with an over six-figure income, a home mortgage with a couple of years already paid off, and traveling the country consulting in high-powered corporate environments.

It was all a facade. Drugs, alcohol, and sex engulfed me. I lived a life I had idealized, but I had not attained real meaning. It was a false, self-created interpretation of reality. I took it to another level. I crossed the line and made choices that affected others greatly. And it put me in jail.

Dysfunction

We, as men, don't always share our struggles—the addictions, the guilt, the perceived shame. American pop culture tells men, "be tough" but pairs this message with images of dysfunctional behaviors. To rise above takes a willingness to seek out the resources required to foster accountability. Most men are in this same boat. I had a first-class seat on that trip.

This cycle of dysfunctional behavior comes to work on autopilot, no thinking involved. We just do, do, do. A mentor told me once, at a deeper level, we as men are looking to fill a void in us, "Our internals are never at peace." We are always attempting to fill our void by any means possible. The words of philosopher Blaise Pascal hit home for me: "What else does this craving, and this helplessness, proclaim but that there was once in man a true happiness, of which all that now remains is the empty print and trace? This he tries in vain to fill with everything around him, seeking solace in things that are not there, the help he cannot find in those that are, though none can help, since this infinite abyss can be filled only with an infinite and immutable object; in other words, by God himself."

I tried to fill a void. I disconnected from those who loved and supported me. I found pleasure in a materialistic lifestyle. I engulfed myself in pleasures, destroying my sense of reality.

Now here I was, sitting in a jail cell reflecting on my actions and their consequences. As quoted from another great and late mentor, "Results... often harsh, always fair."

My journey to being a better man began on that lower bunk ten years ago. I challenge you to take this journey. It has been a fulfilling one for me and has pushed me further beyond what I thought success would look like for me.

Manhood now means taking personal responsibility for my actions, thoughts, and feelings. Manhood is the wisdom to identify the dysfunction in my life and taking the courageous steps to shift to a higher purpose. Manhood means choosing to be a leader in every challenge life brings my way. This is beyond success.

Some of the struggles I've mentioned may resonate with you. If so, know there are others who have been there. Remember, it does not define you!

Rescue

While the journey started in that cell, it took me years to break the destructive thought patterns in my life. I have not "arrived" by any means. As human beings, we are always growing and learning. It required taking an in-depth look at myself and participating in my own rescue. I took responsibility for my poor choices in life, learned empathy, truly knowing and understanding who I am, and walking in that truth with the power to make the right life choices moving forward.

Today, I am a more successful version of the same 25-year-old businessman, with more figures in my income and houses to my name. The outside achievement does not bolster my manhood now. I operate from a flipped mindset, changing me on the inside—making me a better man—leading to higher levels of success and satisfaction then I knew existed.

In 2013, smack in the middle of this journey, I had a life-altering insight. After years of looking at myself in the mirror, day in and day out, God showed me what I am meant to do in this lifetime. My purpose became simple: to help create better men in this world. This journey supersedes success. It's beyond money and toys. To me, becoming the best man I can be leads to true fulfillment. This motivates me. If living my values can influence at least one person become a better version of themselves too, the pain I went through will all be worth it.

Tools

I'm here to tell you poor choices you have made do not define you. True hope exists for your future, beyond the mess. I want to offer you some tools I used along the way:

- Awareness, Awareness, Awareness – I've found it is easy to slip and fall. Awareness anticipates the signals ahead of the curve. Stop. Breathe. Take note of what you are thinking from day-to-day and in your interactions with other people and situations. Experiencing the abundance of negative thoughts during the hard times, gave me the aha, "to think is to create." Get that junk out of your head! What you think of the most will only expand, so take inventory of what you are thinking!
- Open, Responsible Communication – Seek out accountability. I am a believer that men should hold other men accountable. Build a support team around you of men who will lift you up, but are not afraid to call you out on your stuff. To be successful, you must be accountable!
- Prayer – I am a man of faith, and I believe in the power of prayer. Through my journey, prayer has been a significant part of my success. Prayer was and still is an integral part of my success.

Practice

Purpose is the reason for which something exists or is done, made or used. Finding my purpose brought significance to manhood for me.

What is life all about to you?

Why does it matter?

How do you find your purpose?

From my experience, you find it through a great deal of introspection. It starts with awareness, then proceeds into a breakthrough and choice shift.

Here's an exercise that I will leave with you in helping to find your purpose:
1. Take out a blank sheet of paper
2. Write at the top, "What is my true purpose in life?"
3. Write an answer (any answer) that pops into your head. No judgment. The words do not even have to be a complete sentence.
4. Repeat Step 3 until you write the answer that makes you cry. This is your purpose.

This may take you 30 minutes. Or it may take you three months. Or it may take ten years. When you get there, you will know. What purpose will you give your life to moving forward? Grab a hold of that and make it happen. Participate in your own rescue!

Biography

Frank Mbanusi grew up in a household with four younger siblings, raised by a single mother from the age of seven. Through hardships and tragedy, he stepped into manhood very quickly. On this journey, read how he finds purpose beyond success; and walks the path to becoming a better man.

Contact Information

Email: frankmbanusi@gmail.com

Chapter 26

MY DEFINITION OF SUCCESS

By Kadri Kristelle Karu

How do we define success?

Is it a lot of money? A rich lifestyle? A big house? An expensive car? Luxurious trips? Is it enough, or do we need something more to be happy?

Yes, success can be counted like this too. But success could be growing as a person, feeling happy, finding inner peace, having influence, helping others, a happy family life, good health, etc.

Often, we think of ourselves as successful or unsuccessful by comparing ourselves to others. But there is always someone who has more expensive things than we do and there are still people who have less. At times, rich people are unhappy, and financially poor people are happy. Which of them is more successful?

What is success about? Is it equal to a happy life?

When I was in my 20s, I thought I'll be successful living my dream life when I could manage my time effectively, earn good money, live in a beautiful home, have a nice car and travel a lot. During the journey of my life, I added much more of what would qualify as success for me: a happy family life, good friends, positive emotions, good health, helping other people and living a rewarding life by growing and enjoying every minute of life.

It took me years to understand what I really want and what makes me happy. People said I was successful, and I saw all these external things that proved it, but I was not happy. I was looking for my happiness in other people, money, travels, and ended up with an understanding that all we need is self-love. I think people should do whatever it takes to love themselves, live a happy life and encourage others to do the same by being an example. People who value and love themselves are an inspiration for other people.

I was not born into a wealthy family, I grew up with my grandmother, and later saw my mother's struggles with her business, depression, and difficulties. I just wanted to know if there was possibly another way to live, succeed financially, and have fun and enjoy life at the same time.

Now I know by experience that it is possible, and it's based on our own decisions. We can make decisions at every moment of our life; it does not matter where we live or how old we are.

Was it always easy to achieve it? Certainly not. Was it worth it? Absolutely!

I studied in different schools and was looking for what I really like to do. I completed my education at secondary school level, worked in a kindergarten, during studies I worked in a hospital, then trained and worked as a secretary at a bank. I liked the job, but I realized that the most important thing for me was missing – my freedom. So, I decided to study International Business and started to work as a manager and later personnel manager in a big company.

At that time someone showed me options in Network Marketing and direct selling. I was somewhat skeptical about business, but I really liked the products, so I shared my experiences naturally. People grew interested, the company paid me money, and when it was equal to my salary, I thought maybe this is an option to become the hostess of my time and be truly free. I understood by then that I had no good ideas for creating my own business and saw the difficulties in starting ordinary businesses. But I liked the freedom, the teamwork, managing my time myself and the income that Network Marketing allows you to achieve.

When I started, I had a full-time job, my son was three years old, and I just had to find extra time for my Network Marketing business. But I knew what I wanted – freedom. It's wonderful that I've enjoyed direct marketing success for 20 years now and I am really happy about it, it taught me more than what I learned in 5 years of business school. I met many wonderful people, enjoyed great self-development, fantastic travels, freedom, a good income, and these opportunities are limitless.

I am glad to share the experiences I've learned on this fantastic journey. I am still learning but also using the skills I've learned so far because they work in every area of life.

The most important thing I've learned is that you are enough, love yourself and enjoy life! All the advertisements on TV and magazines show us that if we buy this or that we will be better, more beautiful, more complete. It's not true. We are complete as we are and worthy of love. There's nothing bad in good things; it's great to enjoy life, but these fulfill us just for a moment. Very often we think other people need to give us happiness and appreciation. No, it's our job. If we love and appreciate ourselves, others will follow this.

Have a great relationship with yourself, and you will have great relationships with others.

Love yourself; then you can love others and will be loved by others.

We are used to comparing ourselves with others, but we should compare ourselves and our growth with ourselves, this is success.

People are conditioned to live in the past and regret what happened in the past, or they are looking forward to the future where their dreams or fears exist. Life is happening here and now, be present, enjoy it, be curious and open minded.

In being present and curious about life, we can see that life is full of opportunities. Often, we need some courage to catch them, but they are all around us.

People are walking on the street; there is €100 lying on the sidewalk. Many people are passing by without noticing it. Suddenly someone sees it and will pick it up — the same with opportunities around us. There are always opportunities around us. Notice them!

With every opportunity I see, I listen to my intuition; do I have a good feeling about this or not? Even when there is a good feeling, the mind is there, and the fear is pumping up.

It needs courage to deal with it.

My method for this is to figure out as much as I need about this opportunity to be sure, and when it still feels good then make a decision and start. After starting and having made a decision, the fear begins to recede. We have everything we need – the feeling and the information to convince our mind.

On the way, we encounter a lot of people, circumstances and many gifts; we have to be present and see them. The journey is the same or even more important than the destination. Sometimes during the journey, the destination will change, and this is completely okay because during this transition we will be more aware of what we want in life.

Do things that you FEEL you are attracted to, even if your mind is not supportive at this moment. Sometimes our inner voice knows more than our mind. Figure out more about it and don't let your worries sap your energy. If you feel good, you attract positive experiences.

The opportunities are always there, but you cannot see them when you are not opening yourself to them. How do you do it? My question to myself in these situations is: What is the worst thing that can happen?

Our life is all about energy. On some level, we are the sum of the results we achieve. When we are complaining and whining that life is bad, life proves it to us, it's bad, and the opposite is also true. If we feel good, life shows us more good things. This is all about the law of attraction. What helps to raise our energy? Being thankful, doing good things, good music, walking or being in nature, etc. Find out what makes your energy level go higher.

To keep our energy at optimum levels, we need to take care of our physical body too.

Pay attention to moving, nutrition, taking care of your body, and your level of energy will be much higher — the same with our mind. If we don't use it and grow, atrophy will take place. It can be a challenge in the beginning when starting out, but as long as we feel the difference, it's not possible to stop it.

If you feel good, you will attract positive results that will make you feel even better.

When your energy level is low, you can raise it by thinking of things you are thankful for right now.

We take many things in our life for granted until they are not there anymore. So, it's worth appreciating all the time that we have, and there is lots of it. There is a saying, a person is as rich as he (or she) can be grateful for. The person can be wealthy but if he does not appreciate it, then they will always feel it's not enough. There is a secret, be grateful for what you have, and you will have more of what you are grateful for.

Visualization and affirmations.

I've been in many seminars and courses, many tutors have said, write your goals on paper, set the exact date, visualize it and say it to the mirror out loud. I always wrote this suggestion down, but I never did it. Until… One day there was a goal I really wanted. It was the next level in the Network Marketing company I worked for. This title would give me a good income, but more important at that moment, the free luxurious trip to Mauritius with my partner.

It was a huge thing for me at that time.

I was so excited about this opportunity that I would do anything to achieve it. I wrote down the goal, set a date, went to the bathroom and stood next to the mirror. Before that, I was looking around to be sure that I was home alone. I even locked my cat out, then looked to the mirror and said, "I am a Leader." The first few times it was embarrassing, then I just said it, for a while I looked straight to the mirror, and I felt that I AM A LEADER. Finally, I was feeling and acting like the owner of the title; my self-image was changing day by day.

Guess if I took this trip? Yes, I did. This kind of affirmation and visualizing yourself achieving the goal really works.

There is just one BUT... it's better not to stick to our goal if there is a feeling of pressure that the goal is slipping away from you. The great feeling, looking in the mirror, saying in present form: I AM ... and visualizing as we achieve the goal, and then going out and doing your tasks with joy and focusing on helping people, not thinking about our goal but about assisting others.

When we are stuck, we feel pressure, and our energy goes down. People who we are talking to feel it too and it causes a barrier. What should you do when you feel stuck and under pressure? Just take your attention to something else. Go and work out, walk in the natural world, do something different and take yourself off for a while from this action and result. When you feel free about it again, go and act... and have fun with it.

Enjoy every moment of the journey. We set goals, but the most important is what is happening on the way, we may even change our goals when we grow or change the direction, so enjoy.

It's important to be the biggest fan of what you are doing. People can feel it if you are sincere and excited about it, or just scared or unconfident. Action, experiences, knowledge will make you more confident day by day.

Grow, learn from the people who have already achieved what you want to achieve. Seminars, books, webinars, mentors, coaches... there are lots of options you can use for it. Learn and teach what you found out. Teaching is the best way to learn.

Be flexible. Accept that changes are great and happening anyway, whether we want them or not. So be flexible and curious about life.

Investing in self-development is never about wasting time and money. Invest in seminars, books, traveling, etc., and we also need to choose who we listen to. Did they achieve what they are talking about or not, are they experts in this field or just reiterating what they read from books or heard from others. I prefer learning from experts.

We all sometimes feel that things are not going well, but in difficult times we grow the most because we need to find other ways and solutions what we haven't used yet. So, let's play down the difficulties and say to ourselves, "thank you for this opportunity to grow."

Listen to people and add value to their lives. The more we help other people succeed, the more successful we are in turn. If we have authority with people, they listen to us in many areas including what we are doing and the products we are offering.

One thing that is holding us back in achieving success is our comfort zone. Nothing bad about having a rest, but if it lasts too long, it's better to think, didn't I fall back into my comfort zone? Sometimes, we are just thinking and doing nothing; I think we don't need to talk about the importance of actions.

Success is a habit. Make yourself do more things every day and you will get closer to your goals and dreams. If we do something consistently for 40-60 days, it will become habitual. Therefore, we need to do the new habit until we can manage it instinctively.

Look who you are hanging around with. We have, on average, five closest friends. Are they positive, motivated, and encouraging; or are they negative and pessimistic? Who do you want to be? Remember, you will become the average of these five. Choose wisely.

Leave a legacy. Your experiences will help people make better decisions.

Lots of suggestions here, but life is easy. We came here to enjoy it and grow. We can grow by choice or life makes us grow. *Growing by choice is much better.*

Eighty percent of success and happiness is about mindset. Just 20% is about our skills. So we should guard our mindset.

And last, expect miracles and miracles will happen.

Biography

Kadri Kristelle Karu believes there is enough for everyone in this world and we are limitless. If we are ready to learn and grow, we can achieve everything we desire or even something better. Her formula works: **dream-goal-affirmation-plan-learn-act-receive**. The most important thing in life is to *enjoy the journey*.

Contact Information

Website: BeyondSuccesswithKadriKristelleKaru.com
Facebook: https://www.facebook.com/kadri.karu.5
YouTube: https://www.youtube.com/channel/UCDYbU5hYbQuvbZHYoMF798A?view_as=subscriber

Chapter 27

WINNING THROUGH THE WRINKLES IN LIFE

By LaShonda McMorris

On the day you were born, you probably bore your first wrinkle. What? Really? How? We cried for the first few minutes after our birth. Who spanked you? The nurse or the doctor did it to get your lungs working. My understanding now is that doctors no longer use this practice. As babies, we can't verbalize, "Hey, why did you do that?" "What's happening?" or "Hey, that hurts," but our bodies can react. While we experience tears of joy, most tears come from a place of hurt, pain, disappointment or other traumatic experience.

At some point during grade school, you may have been the victim of bullying, teasing you about how you dressed, looked, spoke, what you didn't have, and called names like skinny (I experienced this), fat, dumb, or teacher's pet. You may have even been the contributor to inflicting pain and causing someone else to get a wrinkle. If you haven't had challenges in life, keep living as the saying goes.

Do you remember falling or getting knocked down in the playground? Did you stay on the ground, or did you get up and get over it? Gone through one or more divorces? Lost a job? Had a car accident? Hated with or without a cause, your partner broke off the relationship? Talked about? Lied to? I could go on and on. You reading this chapter is proof that you persevered. Someone will disappoint you, disagree with you, or simply fall out or stop speaking to you, but your pursuit towards your goals, regardless of obstacles, is the sum of persistence.

Not all wrinkles in life are bad because they also shape who you are. Different experiences influence and define your character, faith, motivation, drive, and integrity.

Giving Birth

Nine months of preparation and planning

You have nine months to plan expenses and necessities required for taking care of a baby. Some people can afford to purchase everything in one go, but most people are restricted financially. Planning for your success is likely to be in stages, but do you know what they are? The mother takes the time to write down every item she needs for her baby, similarly to what a wedding planner does for a bride and groom. Planning for your success should be happy times, but during the planning stage, wrinkles could surface too. As famously quoted, which I'm sure you've heard before, "If you can dream it, you can achieve it."

While pregnant with my youngest daughter, I developed Placenta Previa and frequently hospitalized. One night, after a church dinner, I began to experience severe abdominal pain.

My body was discharging something, but my ex-husband at the time prevented me from seeing it. I recall the paramedic saying, "We have a female who has lost a fetus appearing to be 2-3 months old". I remember praying and saying "NOOO Pooh bear (the nickname I initially gave her). Pooh bear you can't go and began to speak life into her. Although the paramedic said one thing, my belief was the opposite. I never saw what my ex-husband or the paramedics saw, but they said I discharged what appeared to be a fetus. The doctors confirmed it was not. My daughter is very much alive, graduated high school class Valedictorian and attending one of the big ten academic alliance universities. This event was one of the biggest wrinkles I had ever experienced in my life, but today all is well.

Babies are in the oven for nine months. That's the period it takes for them to develop all the body parts, organs, and internal makeup before they can be birthed into the world and breathe on their own. Drop any expectations that your success will occur overnight.

Here is the thing, when mommy gets morning sickness, gains then loses weight, the baby doesn't stop developing.

The next step is to plan. You may need additional education/training along the way but be mindful that wrinkles can manifest seemingly out of nowhere. Oh, oh – is there another wrinkle? What do you do? What is your mindset? Remain focused, positive, and motivated. Do not allow depression to creep in or begin feeling sorry for yourself and never start doubting yourself. Before you know it, your first milestone has been achieved, which motivates you to keep moving. Soon after that, you are in warp speed mode and then, oops – another wrinkle. This time you bulldoze right through it and then Walla Success. Celebration time begins! Remember, success, change, or anything New requires you to stay on the path no matter how many wrinkles you experience on your journey.

Time vs. Success

Yes, there is such a thing as a wrinkle when it comes to time and being successful. Time spent unproductively adds little or no value towards your success. Watching television shows all day or sports for hours on end does not add value towards dreams, ideas or goals that were penned on a piece of paper, in a notepad, or on your vision board for years? Now, I am not saying that you can't do these things, nor am I against movies or TV shows, but in the name of all these things that you want to do, how do they help? If several hours are spent daily and weekly talking on the phone about sports, or negative conversation, you are losing valuable time that could have been spent building your network and researching your next steps towards your vision. You need to get yourself closer to taking your business ideas from thought - to life - to action. Does spending hours of your day on Social Media help your idea? To be successful, you need time. If your time isn't managed wisely, you could end up on the phone or on Facebook, telling others how you Could've, Would've, or Should've been a????. Fill in the blank... The enemy of your time are the hours of the day or week doing things that add ZERO value to your ultimate goals and dreams.

Your background and past experiences, good or bad, don't have to affect your future negatively.

When you are knocked down by a life situation, don't just lie there, GET UP! Soldiers in the military are faced with life-and-death situations when the enemy attacks. When soldiers are in training, they train as if the situation is real. It's not a drill or a sequence of practice sessions. Reaching your goals and dreams should be approached as if your life depends on it. Why? If it is not treated as a priority, like "oh, I will get to it later" or "I'll begin writing my play next week" or "planning my new business in a few months when things settle down," it will never get done. I've learned to take action on an idea as soon as it occurs. I haven't mastered the technique yet, but it is something I am more aware of now than ever before. Demand more of yourself because no one else can make you do what needs to be done for your business, invention, education, or coaching program. You get it! Push yourself harder to assure a milestone, a task, etc is completed daily, no matter what!

Be your own success story, pray for something bigger than yourself and for something that's impossible for you to do in your own strength. What and who does your circle include? Are you surrounded by people who know more or less than you? Are they more successful than you? It is essential to increase your network and get to know folks who have made more than you and worked harder than you. If you hang around people who are always talking but not doing, where will you get your energy and support from when you are at a crossroads? Get a mentor. Find someone who inspires you to be a better you and who motivates you into action.

The year 2017 felt like a set up for me. I asked God to surround me with millionaires or those with a millionaire mindset. He did just that. Over the past three years, particularly in the last 12 months, I directly met ten people who are doing great things. And not just doing things to gain personally, but to help communities by giving their time to educate, contribute, share knowledge, wisdom, and skills that enable them to forever be able to FISH for a lifetime NOT just survive for a day.

Utilize your LinkedIn account like a professional showcase. I've seen many profiles that give off the perception that "I'm not really serious" or "I'm just here for kicks, so join me on my road to nowhere." I increased my circle with like-minded professionals, and I don't treat it like a social or hangout club. I don't manage my Facebook page that way either. Value yourself and the information you take in because the bible says, Proverbs 23:7 As a man thinketh in his heart, so is he. Surround yourself with go-getters.

Have you ever felt like, "man, I just can't get this thing, idea, business going" or "how do I start? I don't know what to do." Listen to Podcasts in your arena, get inspiration from others, and read books on the subject.

The Idea

I started my first business in 1990, making and selling jewelry to friends, family, co-workers, and my church family. I thought the products were pretty good only to find that after a few months, the glue that I used caused the jewelry to turn brown in some areas. It's funny how I recall feeling bad and making new pieces for free that did not require glue to compensate the affected customers. I figured, "ok, that didn't work. What else can I do?"

Then in 1995, I joined a company initially selling rendition fragrances door-to-door then opened my own office. I helped ten other people set up their own offices, and then I moved into my own distribution center. With this new role came a new set of challenges or what I consider wrinkles. After two years in business, I had to close the doors because the overhead costs far exceeded the profits. After many other wrinkles and more than 20 years later, I decided to give network marketing another try. My success is inevitable because my mindset shifted from "I can't" to "I will." Take a moment and think about your mindset, do you need a shift?

Do you have any ideas for starting or joining a Network Marketing Program? Do you want to start a business, write a book or play, publish a magazine, start a blog for a Not-For-Profit organization, construction company, or how to become a Ministerial leader? The ideas are endless, so set your goals. Even if what some would consider a failure has become a part of your journey, set them again, refresh them, and seek out what happened in your previous venture. Your success won't come without some teachable moments or experiences to help you grow. Sometimes building a reliable team or customer base can seem never-ending. However, the rewarding part is that you are sharing an opportunity or product that you believe in – otherwise, why else would you do it?

The financial rewards will come as a natural progression of your success. Be proud and don't be afraid when stuff happens. Share those times and ignore what else is said of you. Hey, think of it like this. If the person you share it with has something negative to say, ask them when was the last time they pursued their dreams and goals. Earlier in this chapter, I spoke about who was in your circle. If the right people are in your circle, you can be assured you will get the support and motivation if you fall, "Been there?" "It's ok - go for it again," "You can do it," and all the other encouraging words you need to continue your journey re-energized.

Wrinkled Thoughts are our Greatest Enemy

So, your big idea just sprung a leak, and you're thinking, "how am I going to recover?" "how much will it cost me?" "what will my family think if I don't succeed?." Think about this; what if these highly successful people didn't push forward and tried again after epic failures?

Thomas Edison was told by his teachers that he was 'too stupid to learn anything.'

Sir James Dyson who, after 5,126 failed prototypes for the bagless vacuum cleaner, amassed a net worth of $4.5 billion.

Steven Spielberg was rejected twice.

Walt Disney's editor told him that he 'lacked imagination and had no good ideas.'

Albert Einstein did not start talking until he was four years old.

Jerry Seinfeld was booed and jeered off stage when he froze during his first performance.

The creator of the first Dr. Seuss book was rejected 27 times, yes 27 different publishers, and now he sells more than 600 million copies worldwide.

Oprah Winfrey was fired from her first television job.

Elvis was fired after his first show.

Michael Jordan was cut from his high school basketball team.

All of these folks and many more in our history experienced one or more wrinkles in their lives. Their success came when multiple No's didn't deter them from continuing until they got a Yes. Failures are just wrinkles. Pull out your iron and dream, push, drive, and persist all the way.

Biography

LaShonda McMorris is a passionate communicator, minister, mentor, and empowerment coach. She lives a life of prayer, faith, helping others recognize the winner within them. She has built unforgettable relationships in her professional, ministerial, and personal life over the last 25 years helping people in their personal growth and spiritual development.

Contact Information

Facebook: https://www.facebook.com/MsLaShondaMcMorris
LinkedIn: https://www.linkedin.com/in/lashondamcmorris
YouTube:
https://www.youtube.com/channel/UCAUHzfhvY9wotExiVPbEnmA
Twitter: @LaShondaMcMorris
Instagram: https://www.instagram.com/LaShondaMcMorris

Chapter 28

YOU MIGHT SCREAM, YOU MIGHT CRY, BUT GIVING UP IS NOT AN OPTION

By Magga Sigga

Hello Dear Friend,

I sincerely hope that I am writing to you at a convenient time. I am so happy to reach out to you because I have some news I'd like to share.

If you haven't already guessed, I'm terrible at writing and reading books, but that won't stop me from expressing what I wish to say. I'm terrified of stepping so far out of my comfort zone, and my heart feels like it's going to burst out of my chest because I am so afraid.

Well, I'll give you the news. I am starting to write the first chapter of my book.

No-one would have guessed, not you, not me, or anyone that I know, that one day I would be doing this.

And that is the beauty of it all; given that, if you remember, I am so stubborn. The first thing is I don't often write in English. I read it well, and I have found new ways to do so as time goes on, but this has taken so much more time than I thought. Every sentence is a challenge, but I hope that my message remains clear.

I think back to my preschool teacher. He spent three years trying to teach me how to read and write. For most of the time, this appeared a near-impossible task, until one day he asked me, "Are you so stubborn that you have decided you simply cannot read or write?"

I sat there, my eyes filled with frustrated tears. I could not understand this. I had no idea how this is going to be possible because the letters basically seemed to drift right off the page, and I had no idea how to put them back, let alone the order in which they should be placed.

Then he told me that I could do this if I truly wanted to. I sat there with a huge question mark written across my face,

"How in the world am I going to do this?"

Well, I found a way. I made the decision that I could read, and I would spend countless hours mastering this essential skill. At the age of 10, I was finally able to write my own name. And that was my first victory.

However, despite these gains, I soon decided that school wasn't for me and that I would run away from home. I didn't actually run away, I just talked to my mama and said I'm not doing the formal education thing. I'm just not cut out for it. I was confident that I could find work, and I did, I started working at a fish factory.

Even then I was confident that I would be successful if I worked hard enough, and so I did.

At 23 years of age, I made another decision that would change my life. I decided to put the money aside, quit working all my different jobs, and go back to school. I had been in school for six weeks before I went to the headmaster and admitted my problem. I told him that I had to leave because I was so stupid that I couldn't read and write. Just like my preschool teacher, he didn't believe me. Once again, I had a teacher who had faith in me. However, this one asked me to take a few tests for my reading skills, and I found out that I was dyslexic. I had struggled for so long, and I finally knew why. Knowing this, my headmaster continued to teach me how to read and write while catering to the challenges caused by my dyslexia. I was finally able to read and get the grades I was capable of achieving.

This was true self-esteem.

The most difficult part of my dyslexia is miss-spelling words. It was so easy for other people to notice, and, for a time, led to people bullying and underestimating me. Of course, I didn't like that, but I managed to not to give in to hate and anger and worked hard to improve myself despite the criticism.

I know everyone is facing something challenging, and I know everyone has their own problems, and most people just need some help to feel confident in themselves. I soon decided that I wasn't going to be bitter. Growing up with these issues, I learned something I believe had helped me greatly. That's something I want to pass on to you. I bet there is something on your mind and I guess that you might be looking for a way forward.

The first thing I want to tell you, my dear friends, is that you are capable and you have something in your heart that will allow you to overcome these challenges. I know for sure that if I had known about my dyslexia earlier, I would have been able to receive suitable help for my reading difficulties. I know that then my life would be much different today.

I'm not willing to waste my time on regrets. Instead, I would recommend you actively explore the fear and see what is lurking there.

It's okay to cry, it's okay to scream, but it's never okay to give up.

I will now take you to the year 2010.

I've now started a family. I have my daughter; she is my youngest. I have two boys: the oldest is 30, and the youngest is 20, and they have both grown into amazing men.

My daughter was born on the 24th week of the pregnancy. She was quite small, only 31.5 cm and 530 g (12 inches, 1.2 lbs). We spent four months in the ICU, not knowing how things would turn out.

As you can imagine, this was a very stressful time for my entire family, and then, finally, when she got to come home, it started to be a very stressful time for me personally. I thought it would be a good idea to simply give up on sleep entirely so that I can take care of my daughter. Let me tell you; it's never a good idea. But when kids are used to waking up every two hours, it is quite difficult to stop doing it.

So instead of sleeping through the night, I just stayed awake. After about a year and a half of this I was so tired and feeling completely run down and exhausted; in a state of near total burn-out.

The time that I was taking care of my daughter I wasn't taking care of myself. I put on a lot of weight and my health suffered.

I also struggled to take financial care of my family, but I was in luck. I started in the network marketing business. In the industry, there is immense pressure for constant self-improvement and development. And that was exactly what I did.

You might have noticed that I'm a fighter, I don't give up easily. I started walking, swimming, and paying attention to my diet. I started attending a health care institution to work on myself. I noticed that I had developed a negative mindset. It was blocking my career progress, and it was diminishing my energy. I was no longer a positive person. So I started listening to podcasts that helped fix what was broken: to start building myself up to the stubborn fighter I used to be. I don't know if I was actually walking because I needed to walk or if I needed that physical discipline to change the way I was thinking and avoid negative, cyclical thoughts.

After so many years, I made another life-changing decision. I would change the world around me instead of trying to change who I was. That is what I have done. I choose what I'm listening to. I choose the people I spend time with. There are so many quality podcasts and YouTube channels and everything out of there, so many people spreading these great positive messages that it could be very difficult to choose the best one.

I recently had a talk with my cousin. We discussed living in fear, and I was explaining to her that you don't have to drive all around the country just to have the courage to go to the grocery store, you just have to take a little step every single day and go from there. You will grow and eventually you will be at the place that you have always dreamed of being.

I then decided that I didn't want to be afraid of heights anymore and that, despite my vertigo, I will go up the mountain, literally and metaphorically. That took me about four years! I desperately needed that feeling winning once more - of succeeding at something that made me feel great. I needed to know that my inner warrior was still there. I needed to rebel, so I decided to welcome the fear.

The trail started slowly, and soon we were halfway up the mountain. I sat down as I thought it would now be a good time to have a stress-busting cigarette, but I had given up smoking three years ago. That wasn't an option. I sat down and cried my eyes out as I was so afraid of becoming lost.

And I thought of the rescue team not being able to find me.

But I didn't want to go down; I wanted to go up. I knew that if I wanted to save someone I wanted to go up. I trained as an EMT basic for a long time, so I knew that saving someone else would get me there.

And so I did. I finally stood at the top of the mountain with the feeling that I was a winner coursing through my veins.

I knew that I had changed my inner direction. I knew that I had created the feeling of victory inside my heart once more. I knew that I wasn't afraid anymore and that on the other side of fear is freedom.

My dear friend, I am going to leave you with the words 'take care.'

And to me that means you are special, you are unique, and you have something no one else has.

And my dear friends, you are capable.

Biography

Magga Sigga is an Entrepreneur, ACC-ICF Life-Coach and an Influencer. Her strength is her inner power. She believes in people's greatness and helps them reach their goals in life. She is brave and ready to go where others do not dare.

Contact Information

Facebook: https://www.facebook.com/margret.jons
Twitter: @MARSIR Jons
Instagram: margret.jons

Chapter 29

THE 5 PRINCIPLES OF NETWORKING

By Nicholas Arbutina

While contemplating the opening chapter for this book, I wanted to focus on a topic that would benefit anyone in a networking company anywhere in the world so I can add value in helping them build a successful business. In other words, I want to share a strategy based on principles that have stood the test of time. Many of the tactics may change with technology, social media, etc., but the real fundamentals of this business remain as true today as they did 50 years ago.

So, after digging deep and reviewing what I learned, there is one teaching in particular, that I want to share. My mentor gave me advice that has added tremendous value to our business and team. It is based on the 5 Principles of Networking, or what I like to call, the 5 P's. I am going to illustrate how these principles relate to my business, health and wellness, but can be applied to any business model in the networking industry.

The 5 Principles are: People, Purpose, Process, Products, and Perseverance. As mentioned, I will detail how these principles apply to my business, which can be prioritized differently according to your needs and your business. Consider how these principles affect your business and the products or services that you offer. For example, if Products are more important than your business Process, then switch them around. Use these 5 Principles to guide your leaders most effectively and efficiently as possible.

PEOPLE - People First is core value #1, so I will focus on that first. Without people, you have no business. Let me say that again, WITHOUT PEOPLE YOU HAVE NO BUSINESS. People are the number one asset, whether they are your customers, discount buyers, or team builders; people make up the entire business. So, if you don't like people, I hate to tell you that you probably shouldn't be in this business.

But I say that with mixed feelings because truthfully when I started my business, I was an overworked, traditional business owner who was owned by his business. I was so frustrated with customers and employees that I felt that I no longer liked people. But I knew deep down that I loved people and had allowed society and my emotions to get the better of me. I knew I had to make a change, or it would cost me everything in the long run.

So, I made people my priority and started to love working with and for people. Whether it was helping them achieve physical, emotional, financial, relationship, spiritual, or mental goals, I wanted to help people DO LIFE BETTER. If I could give credit to one person who helped change it for me, it was a friend that I will call Stephanie. She was a stressed out, overweight, middle-aged woman who had lost her love of life. I did not know Stephanie until she joined my team and I watched her transform into an amazing woman, mom, and leader. Through her journey, she lost over 140 lbs and became a better mom, wife, and business partner. She even won several international level transformation bikini contests. Had it not been for the changes I helped her with and the potential I could see in Stephanie, I may still be stuck in my "business owning me mentality." Thank you, Stephanie!

PURPOSE - Purpose is essentially as important as people, because if you don't have a STRONGER THAN OAK "WHY" then you probably won't succeed in this business either. Your WHY must be what pushes you through the tough times because there will be tough times. As every thought leader on the planet will tell you: "Your Why has to make you Cry." I wholeheartedly believe that because you will encounter adversity. You will lose friends, possibly family; you will be called crazy, you will be ridiculed and even laughed at. So, find your purpose and use it to fight through the tough times.

Truthfully, you should not have to think about your WHY. It should be a feeling inside you that makes you want to RULE THE WORLD or achieve greatness. We all have greatness in our God-given potential. You need to discover how to unleash that greatness, and it all starts with your purpose.

And don't worry if your WHY changes. It will most likely evolve because as you grow and develop, so will your priorities, goals, and outlook on life. Personally, my WHY has constantly evolved as I have evolved. When I first started my business, my WHY was to regain my health, so I could see my girls grow up. Then, when I accomplished that, it evolved into being more involved in their lives and then wanting to retire myself from my business. As I achieved my original purpose from the networking business, I continued to grow bigger WHYs. Through this evolution, something amazing begins to develop. You realize that when you started this journey, you were most likely shooting for SUCCESS, but as you achieve more WHYs and serving a purpose, you begin to become SIGNIFICANT. And once you've ACHIEVED SIGNIFICANCE, SUCCESS WILL NEVER BE ENOUGH! As I sit here writing this book, I am accomplishing my evolving WHY.

PROCESS – This principle will vary depending on your company, the type of business, and the products or services, or both. The Process refers to how your company does business. Most of your process will be about how your corporate staff or accomplished leaders promote your business. This will be through different tools such as videos, graphics, or comparison charts – whatever materials your company has put together for you to use from the back office, as well as for front-facing services that include one-on-one, in-home parties, meetings, or hotel rooms.

The great thing about the process is that there is no one way to go about promoting your business, as it helps to have a diversified toolbox at your disposal. Sometimes, a one-on-one with a close friend is ideal, at other times, a hotel meeting could be more suitable and sociable for when the CEO is in town. No matter what your company's preferred method, make sure you show up and commit to the process. There is an old saying that I like on both ends of the spectrum: "Sometimes you need the meeting, while other times the meeting needs you."

For example, we are pioneering a movement with the world's first ever customized vitamin platform. So, the validity of our company and our core product is based on a free online health assessment. To keep this simple, our mainstream PROCESS is to JUST TAKE THE ASSESSMENT or #JTTA. Our whole business is based around our assessment. Not only does the assessment recommend a vitamin program based on 3rd party, independent, peer-reviewed clinical studies, but it also recommends our lifestyle products (we'll discuss products in the 4th P) On a lighter note, while coming up with our PROCESS, one of our leader's said let's make it #JTTFA, and everyone looked at him like WHAT? He said, "What's wrong with JUST TAKE THE FREE ASSESSMENT!" Just commit to your company's process because there is an objective behind it. It works!

PRODUCTS - There is a reason for leaving Products close to the end. Without products, most companies would not be in business because Products (or services) are the backbone of almost every business. Products are of paramount importance, and every company has them, so in networking, you must believe that your products are the BEST.

Your firm BELIEF in your products will keep you going when you start questioning your sanity. And you will question your sanity, or sometimes you may question network marketing, your company, your upline, your downline, or anyone, and everyone. So, make sure that you are passionate about your products. Make sure that you are a product of the product. You don't have to be the product expert but you will need to know how each of your products work, and there is no better way than using them yourself.

To add value for people, accurately assess the client's needs to determine which product you will recommend that will help and serve its purpose. But, how do you do that? Ask questions. Remember, networking is a social business, and you don't just want to sell products transactionally, you want to fill a need transformationally. In other words, you don't just want to sell for the sake of selling by getting someone to spend their hard earned money; you want to help them DO LIFE BETTER in an area where your products can benefit them.

PERSEVERANCE - This is the big one and why it is saved for last. Without perseverance, you could have the other 4 p's completely mastered and yet you would not survive in network marketing. Perseverance is what will keep you motivated after your tenth consecutive NO, or after your mother tells you you're crazy, or your oldest friend laughs at you and says you have joined a cult.

Perseverance is what will keep you from doing the absolute no-no in network marketing, and in life: QUITTING.

"Just Don't Quit" are the words I always remember from the late, great Mark Yarnell. No matter what you do, JUST DON'T QUIT! Whether you are part-time or full-time, quitting is a sure way to fail. If doing it part-time, it will take many more years to succeed, but if you consistently do something to move your business forward every day, you will see growth.

Believe me. I speak from experience. There were many times I considered quitting, the times when I lost my best associate and their entire leg, or when the new "Rock Star" never sponsored a single person, or when a leader stole a prospect. If you don't quit, you will most likely experience all these situations and more. The only constant is the belief in YOURSELF!

Your belief in yourself is what will keep you from quitting. As you continue to grow, hopefully from as many books like this that you read, you can also develop into a leader. As the foremost authority on leadership, John Maxwell, says in the Law of Victory "Quitting is Unthinkable!" That must be your mindset from the beginning. I think what helped me fight through those tough times is having a clear vision of the BIG PICTURE – your ultimate goal. Set your sights, as lofty as they may be, on where you want to be in 5 or 10 years, and just don't quit. At the beginning of your business, (and I know it sounds hard to believe, especially if you've struggled), but persevering and remaining consistent will power you through the hard times to see that light at the end of the tunnel.

Next, I will illustrate how to tie all five principles together. Stephen Covey describes Habit 7 in The Seven Habits of Highly Effective People as Sharpen the Saw, or, sharpen twice and cut once. This is the basic habit of honing your skills. Learn to master each of the five principles: Get to know and love PEOPLE, find your WHY and never lose sight of it. Learn your company's PROCESS and share it with unwavering passion and faith. Become a PRODUCT of the product and represent your company with pride, and PERSEVERE through the good and the bad.

I hope you can see how these five principles will help you succeed in any networking business. While each principle plays a vital role in the success of your business, an understanding of how they all come together is of utmost importance. You really can't have one without the other four. You could probably succeed with only one or two of the principles for a short period, but to sustain growth over an extended period, you will ultimately need to apply all five of these principles. Isn't that why we are all in this business? To have long term success growing an enormous team by applying certain principles over a long period. But if there was one piece of advice, I want to pass on that helped me through the hard times is "JUST DON'T QUIT."

Biography

As a contractor who wanted more out of life, Nicholas Arbutina has transformed his life into one of significance. Through personal growth, he has a passion for helping people DO LIFE BETTER. But his greatest accomplishment is the legacy that he is leaving for his children.

Contact Information

Facebook: https://www.facebook.com/nick.arbutina.7
LinkedIn: https://www.linkedin.com/in/nickarbutina/
YouTube:
https://www.youtube.com/channel/UCfqmXRPmO80VP-CJwSsV86g
Twitter: https://twitter.com/ArbutinaNick
Instagram: https://www.instagram.com/nickarbutina/

Chapter 30

TRIUMPH THROUGH A BUMPY ROAD

By James Mbele

"Awareness is like the sun; when it shines on things, they are transformed." ~ Nhat Hanh

Have you ever asked yourself why some people live a luxurious life and why they attract almost all their heart's desires, while others barely make it? It's a question I used to ask myself growing up.

"The moment of enlightenment is when a person's dreams of possibilities become images of probabilities. Nothing in this world brings ecstasy into a dreamer's life than to see the most cherished images in his mind and heart transformed into something tangible." – **Vic Braden.**

As you go through this book, you will understand that you have done yourself a great favor by investing in one of your greatest assets; "**You.**" It's my honest desire that as you read this book, your mind will be renewed and transformed.

I grew up in a remote rural village coming from very humble beginnings, but, of course, like any other child, I had big dreams and always imagined a great life for myself and my family. Life was hard then, and we were just surviving, for even a simple meal was hard to come by and more often than not, we were forced to beg for food from our relatives.

My high school principal, **Father O'Toole,** saw greatness in me and pointed out to my dad that I was called to transform lives, and that has been the pillar of my life. "If one advances confidently in the direction of his dreams and endeavors to live the life which he has imagined, he will meet with success unexpected in common hours." **– Henry David Thoreau**.

I had dreams of living a luxurious life. While in employment, I specialized in marketing through the Chartered Institute of Marketing (CIM) – UK. I qualified as a chartered marketer. Demand for salespeople with my qualifications was high, so job offers were plentiful. I finally landed a role in a company which had branches in several countries, and this provided me the opportunity to travel to different cities in Africa and overseas.

However, as an employee, I didn't have time and financial freedom, and it dawned on me that I might never realize my dreams of bigger and better things in life. I knew that for me to live the creative vision for my future, I had to break out of my comfort zone. As the famous quote states, "**opportunity meets the prepared**." I was so ready for change, and that's when I met a friend who introduced me to the world of multilevel marketing.

The first day I attended their presentation, I was mesmerized by the tuition given by the person who had invited me. It opened me up to a world of possibilities just by listening to the testimonials of the speakers. We learned how to leverage on people, and I was excited beyond belief. I saw my dreams come alive that day.

The income levels of the top earners in this network marketing company shocked me. I was however patient enough to remain in full-time employment while doing part-time network marketing. At this point, I knew I had to *do* more to *become* more, and that's when I started reading books and watching videos from top speakers.

I now wanted to achieve a much higher income and decided to research the best strategies to apply to this end. I looked for the top earners in the network marketing industry, and I was shocked to learn that some of them were even earning one million dollars monthly.

I had to act fast; I consulted Google for the secrets applied by these top earners. I gathered a wealth of knowledge by reading countless books and watching a huge number of videos produced by the world's top motivational speakers, such as Tony Robbins, Les Brown, Jim Rohn, Randy Gage, and Matt Morris, among others.

Within five months, I qualified for overseas trips with this part-time job, my income increased tremendously, and my presentation skills improved enormously, and it was time to 'fire' my boss. At that moment, my childhood dream of owning a car came true.

A Chinese proverb says, "Studying is like sailing against the current. A boat must forge ahead, or it will be swept downstream." I was competing with my goals by attending all the company events and seminars within my country and abroad. I never missed a single training opportunity. I also had acquired the skill of inviting prospects to business presentations. The secret to success became easy to find, you only need to look for successful people in your line of business and do what they do, and within a short period, you will be successful.

Within two-and-a-half years in network marketing, I had a team of 10,000 leaders in Africa. By this time, I became a sought-after leader by various network marketing companies globally. Word spread like wildfire of how influential I was, and many business owners wanted me to lead their organizations.

Being a leader, I took up the role of investing in my business partners and bookings for meetings and catering for all expenses. I would pay for halls and spend the whole day inviting people for meetings through social media and word of mouth, and most people confirmed their attendance. One day while in my own country, I called a meeting and, with excitement, I drove with my son to the meeting's destination armed with all the necessary materials. Upon arrival, my son went straight into setting up the projector and arranged the tables and seats. At that time, no one had arrived for the meeting, "it's still early," I would tell myself. So I imagined it would only be a matter of time and guys would start showing up any second, and besides the African Leader (myself) is here! No one would miss this training opportunity; I would chest-beat.

One leader came after one hour of waiting, and late, two others came. Disappointment started slowly setting in, I encouraged myself, and I rose up from my seat, took the mic, and began to teach the three gentlemen and my son. I was shouting at the top of my voice. I refused to allow the low turnout to dictate my mood. I trained them for hours, and later we all went back home satisfied. I learned from the best; my mentors taught me never to give up because of the low turnout on my presentations. It's never about quantity, but rather the quality of the leaders you produce.

"Read the biographies and autobiographies of great people, and again you discover that each of these people went through setbacks many times." stated **David J. Schwartz**. However, through focus, consistency, vision, and persistence, you will get there in the end. I remember one time promoting a business while in Nigeria, and it did not go well, finances were not flowing, and paying for accommodation and meals proved difficult. I even thought of looking for a job. However, my dreams were much bigger than mere employment. As **Robert Schuler** would say; "TOUGH TIMES NEVER LAST BUT TOUGH PEOPLE DO"; tough as it was my strong desires made me overcome the challenge.

I had to pick up the pieces and move on. I believe when we look at the length of life, greatness begins with our inner attitude irrespective of whatever level we can find ourselves in. Great people have great attitudes even in doing small things. I teach my audiences, "Traits of Millionaires", including Attitude, Learning from the Past and Never Giving Up, among others. I knew it was time to apply them in real life. I came across an audiotape by **Matt Morris** on "7 Secrets to 7 Figures," which I listened to religiously, making me rise against all odds to cross the boundaries of social mediocrity.

Dreams can take you to territories far beyond your comfort zone, **Goethe** once said; "Dream no small dreams for they have no power to move the hearts of men." Just as the fetus develops in the womb, dreams also develop as we grow older; my dreams grew so big they scared me. I needed to refuel, re-strategize, and work even more smartly for my new aspirations.

Given my good reputation and integrity, I was sought-after by another company. I took the lead as the coach and business was booming, money started flowing in, and I was able to pay all my outstanding bills, and my lifestyle changed drastically.

I was gaining popularity, and I quickly expanded my network of trusted partners in many parts of Africa and Asia. Life became fun; flying to different places, holidaying with my family. It was also at this time I was able to move houses from a middle-class environment to a home on a leafy suburb near the city center which I paid for in cash. I now drive my dream cars, and I have elevated my parents and my siblings' lifestyles.

"Change your focus from making money to serving more people, and more money will come," said **Robert Kiyosaki**. I have shifted my focus into touching lives and empowering others for the world remembers people who gave their lives for the welfare of others through unconditional love and service.

The sweetest and biggest adventure you can take is to live the life of your dreams. Nothing compares to living a fulfilled life of not only accomplishing most or all your dreams and living beyond success by making the world a better place. Being able to turn failures, setbacks, ridicule, and past mistakes into victories are the greatest weapons we can possess in the world of business and all areas of our lives.

According to the author **Willie Jolley**, "a setback is a set up for a comeback." I have gone through setbacks that were to damage me and my reputation seriously but, as a result of reading books and listening to top motivational speakers, I learned to learn from disappointments, grow from them and bounce straight back.

I believe that after reading this book, your life will be transformed and that your perspective on life will change. You are well equipped to face life again with more determination, and confidence with new dreams in your mind and a higher standard of self-belief.

One thing I know for sure is that God's intentions for us go beyond anything we can imagine. The truth is that you are powerful beyond comprehension, beyond measure, and that you can be anything you want. I am a living testimony of this. I made up my mind growing up never to settle for anything less in life than my destiny.

I dare you to start finding that greatness within you. If we nurture our human spirit, it can explore the deepest depths of human potential. We are all born winners regardless of our religion, race, status, or background. The only difference is who we become is the choices we make in life.

Onwards! Decide to hunt down your dreams and beat them mercilessly into submission.

Exploit the talents and gifts given to you freely by your Creator and do not allow any limiting beliefs to hinder you from achieving your dreams.

Always create time every day for meditation, be honest in all your endeavors, be generous in everything you do, compliment others, and avoid giving criticism. Avoid procrastination by all means and face your fears with boldness. There is no future in the past, so don't dwell on it.

Set your goals promptly and follow them through. Make sure your goals are massive and write them down. Keep the company of like-minded people.

I have followed all these tips to the letter, and I have managed to climb the ladder of success, it's my prayer that you will be transformed too.

Biography

James Mbele's career in sales and marketing spans various companies in Africa and abroad. He earned his chartered marketer certification from the UK's Chartered Institute of Marketing, applying his expertise for more than seven successful years as an entrepreneur in the direct sales and network marketing industry.

From humble beginnings in Kenya, James Mbele's enormous potential and willingness to help others was first recognized by his high school principal, Father O'Toole. To this day, he's remained true to his philanthropic calling to inspire others to rise to their highest potential.

Rising quickly in this global arena and traveling to more than fifty countries to speak and motivate others, his service above and beyond the call of duty has been rewarded with numerous accolades. His visionary leadership has mentored many around him to experience massive success in business and life.

He is married to Christine since 1994. They are blessed with a son, Brian, and a daughter, Linnet.

Contact Information

Website: https://jamesmbele.com/

Chapter 31

RULE YOUR MIND, ROCK YOUR BEST LIFE

By Steph Shinabery

"Awareness is like the sun; when it shines on things, they are transformed." ~ Nhat Hanh

Dr. Victor Lord Oliver was my Zoology professor in college. He was an interesting guy. He showed us vinegar eels, which are actually nematodes (worms) in the vinegar and he then swallowed a dropper full from a pipette. Got to love a scientist. One of the things I remember him saying more accurately than the topic on the *stratification of epithelial tissue* is: "if you watch what you think, you won't have to watch what you say."

I contemplated this deeply, and it wasn't until years later when I understood that my thoughts create my results. My thoughts create my reality.

I had a life-changing event that forced me to evaluate my thinking patterns and learn to practice awareness of thought. Awareness is a gift because you miss so much when you go through life on autopilot. I am fascinated with the brain, the mind, neuroplasticity, habits, and the biology of thought as it relates to human potential.

Watch your thoughts; they become words. Watch your words; they become actions. Watch your actions; they become habits. Watch your habits; they become character. Watch your character; for it becomes your destiny. ~ Upanishads

---

"Scar tissue is stronger than regular tissue. Realize the strength, move on." ~ Henry Rollins

Kintsugi is a Japanese art form where broken or cracked ceramic vessels are repaired with gold instead of being discarded. Its flaws are strengthened, celebrated, accentuated, and honored instead of disguised. Human flaws give us character as well, and they can become our strengths and should be celebrated.

My brain is not normal. Many of my friends and most of my colleagues are not aware of this as I haven't shared it publicly, due to the stigma it carries. People still whisper about this sort of thing and pass judgments. Because of this attitude and mindset, people continue to suffer in silence. I know because I was afraid to seek help.

Those days were a dark hole of depression for me, feelings of despair, and impending doom was not uncommon. I felt at any moment, my world would crumble. I was wrecking my health, my relationships, and I felt empty inside. I looked in the mirror and could not recognize who was looking back. I was a shell of a body; just hanging on, swearing tomorrow would be different, tomorrow I would have the resolve I needed. That's a lonely place to be.

There was a period in my life when I realized my drinking was abnormal, but I was stumped. I couldn't figure out how I could have so much willpower in so many areas of my life, but absolutely no control over my drinking. I could endure pain and suffering when it came to pushing my body to its physical limits. I ran marathons and ultra-marathons. I pushed myself with round-the-clock adventure racing. Being tired, cold, and even lost, but still, I pressed on. I was disciplined in my studies and my work. But alcohol had me whipped. Despite understanding the harmful effects of this progressive and fatal disease if left untreated, I felt I was losing the battle. Fortunately, I had that moment when I said enough is enough, and I was able to get help.

Eventually, this disease will become known for what it is, a disorder of the brain, of altered cognition, instead of a character defect. We don't have to whisper about heart disease or diabetes, and we shouldn't have to whisper about addiction. With addiction, just as with any disease, once you understand that you have it, you need to take responsibility for the treatment of it. Fortunately, I was able to do that, and it turned my life around.

Scientists have now pinpointed the exact areas of the brain that are involved namely, the *nucleus accumbens* (reward circuit), *anterior cingulate cortex* (impulse control), *basal forebrain* and the *amygdala* to name a few. They accurately understand the areas of the brain affected and have been able to do experimental treatments for addiction with pulses of electromagnetic wave therapy to the pre-frontal cortex, and it worked! I like to use the scientific names as it seems hard to say you have a moral failing in your nucleus accumbens or to place judgment on your amygdala, but you can say that your anterior cingulate cortex failed you.

Due to the neuroplasticity of our brain, new neural networks can be formed. With abstinence, implementation of new practices and behavior modification, addiction can be treated. You change your brain with new thoughts and new habits, just as you can with anything in your life that you want to change.

"We are constantly invited to be who we are." ~ Henry David Thoreau

I believe if I would have understood that my thoughts create my reality, the importance of tuning into my intuition and using my emotions as a guide to being on the right track, my career would have been on a different trajectory.

When I went off to college, I thought I wanted to coach basketball and teach physical education. In my first physical education class, I quickly realized it wasn't for me.

I discovered art and science. I fell in love with creativity and spent hours in the studio. I loved putting marks on paper and giving thoughts and ideas a three-dimensional life. It still amazes me that our physical world was first "made up" in our heads. I wanted to find a way to earn a living as an artist. Mom was encouraging me to stick with the sciences. You know, something I could get a job in. It became my belief system that it was unlikely I could make a living as an artist.

I was majoring in biology and had a wild idea about becoming a marine biologist and swimming with sharks. That summer, I took a diving class so I could spend a semester at the ocean studying marine life. I couldn't descend past 10 feet as I was unable to equalize the pressure in my ears due to childhood scar tissue from ruptured eardrums. I marked marine biology off my list.

In my fourth year of college, I was still trying to figure out my path. If you were following this narrative on a visual timeline, this is the spot I would emphasize with a red sharpie: here is where I became a conformist. I bought into the conventional wisdom of having to pick a career with health insurance benefits, 401K. Work for forty years and then collect your retirement. That was my plan.

This would have been a good time for me to sit down and write; do some soul searching to examine what was holding me back. What do I want in my life? What do I love to do? What experiences do I want to have and what contributions do I want to make to the world? That's not what happened because, after four years of college, I felt I needed to hurry up and figure it out.

I applied and was accepted to nursing school. I graduated and first went to work in a Burn Unit, then a Trauma Unit. About a year into my nursing career, I knew I didn't love it. I stayed in the field for years, spending most of my time working in Intensive Care Units. Making changes can be uncomfortable. Comfort, or not being able to sit in discomfort, can be a killer of dreams.

While I didn't love my career as a nurse, life was still good. The schedule I worked afforded me opportunities to do some awesome things with my time, and I got in crazy good shape. I went back and finished that art degree in printmaking and sculpture. I have had my art displayed in shows, a sculpture garden, university, and in personal collections.

Shortly after finishing my art degree, I went back to graduate school for anesthesia. I was 42. I love the variety, and I love the mix of physiology, pharmacology, and compassion that I get to utilize every day. It took most of my adult life to get into a career where I was happy to jump up and go to work.

I'm still writing my story. My career is still evolving. I have a passion for helping others reach their highest potential. I love having a conversation with someone and seeing the light bulb go off when they have that AHA moment of "I can do this!" or "why not me" or "why not now." I have often heard people say they have always wanted to "x," or they felt there was something else they were meant to do. Yet, they ignored that voice and continued to settle for where they are because of fear or limiting beliefs. Be willing to get uncomfortable; it's where the magic happens.

Vishen Lakhiari is one of today's thought leaders. Through his company Mindvalley, he has a program called Conscious Engineering. He interviews other thought leaders and game changers from around the globe. One of the questions he asks all of them is, "what gets you out of bed in the morning?" I love that question. We should all strive to do work that makes us want to jump out of bed in the morning.

"The authentic self is the soul made visible." ~ Sarah Ban Breathnach

Listen to that voice inside, it knows. It is the universe nudging you to your greatness. There is always a next level in you. Lean into it and cultivate your passions as that is where you will decode your genius and find your gift to the world. Be authentic; celebrate your Kintsugi. When you show up authentic, it paves the way for others to do the same.

I believe if we gave people the tools they needed at an early age to maximize their human potential, we would see a happier, healthier, and more productive society. I believe we should introduce a 'success for living' toolbox to the school systems to teach kids the power of thought and teach them how to think. Socrates said, *"To find yourself, think for yourself."* You know, conscious engineering.

"In order to succeed, we must first believe that we can." ~ Nikos Kazantzakis

Success starts in the mind. Success is brought to life through persistent focus and action. It is bringing value to the lives of those around you. It is waking up with gratitude for what you do and knowing that you are having a positive impact on the world.

Rule your mind, or it will rule you. If you feel there is some passion or vocation calling you, there is. Go for it! Work on changing your inner dialogue if it is not serving you. Lean into the uncomfortable. Put these four A's on your radar: awareness, authenticity, attitude, and action.

You have infinite potential. It is never too late to open a new chapter in your life. You get to write your life story. Jim Rohn said, "you have two choices: you can make a living, or you can design a life."

I'll end with this quote from Paul Arden, who said, "You need to aim beyond what you are capable of. You need to develop a complete disregard for where your abilities end. Make your vision of where you want to be a reality. Nothing is impossible."

Biography

Steph Shinabery is a Certified Registered Nurse Anesthetist, business coach, and entrepreneur. She is helping people transform their business and lives through cultivating practices and habits that upgrade mindset, focus, clarity, energy, and systems for success. She works with network marketing professionals to leverage social media marketing to grow their business.

Contact Information

Facebook: https://www.facebook.com/steph.shinabery
LinkedIn: https://www.linkedin.com/in/steph-shinabery-966457176/
Twitter: https://twitter.com/pedalart
Instagram: https://www.instagram.com/stephshinabery/

www.ingramcontent.com/pod-product-compliance
Lightning Source LLC
Chambersburg PA
CBHW020649220526
45464CB00001B/363